MEN WHO DARED
IN BIBLE TIMES

by Grace W. McGavran

TEACHER'S BOOK
A Co-operative Vacation School Text
for use with Junior
Boys and Girls

WILDSIDE PRESS

CONTENTS

MEDITATION

I sought the Lord, and afterward I knew
He moved my soul to seek him, seeking me;
It was not I that found, O Saviour true,
No, I was found of thee.

Thou didst reach forth thy hand and mine enfold;
I walked and sank not on the storm-vexed sea,—
'Twas not so much that I on thee took hold,
As thou, dear Lord, on me.

I find, I walk, I love, but, O the whole
Of love is but my answer, Lord, to thee,
For thou wert long beforehand with my soul,
Always thou lovedst me.

—Anonymous

A WORD TO YOU

God has something to say to us!

These days of study ahead will help us find out about ways in which God revealed himself to some of the great leaders of Bible times who responded to his will for them, thus becoming sources of strength to their people and instruments of God's purpose for mankind.

As juniors identify with Bible characters to whom God revealed himself, and through whom he worked, they may come to a deeper appreciation of the Bible. They may see it as a means of God's revelation and find in it his purpose for us today.

You are one of the people through whom God is working today. You will have a thrilling time. You will find yourself growing as the children whom you lead grow.

You have help. The Bible through which God speaks is the greatest help. This textbook which describes experiences others have had with juniors is another help. Then there are your workers and as many other helps as you can gather in your mind and heart. Start right now looking at what your first day holds for you and the children.

We, too, can be among those whom God can use to carry forward his will and his purpose for the children who are to be in our group for this vacation church school.

The Author

INTRODUCTION

THE PURPOSE OF THE COURSE

This course of study for juniors is in the area of "Our Bible Heritage." It is planned to help boys and girls use the Bible to learn about seven major Bible characters and how God chose them to fulfill certain purposes in his plan for mankind. Enough of the setting of the life and times of each character is given to help boys and girls see the men as real persons with everyday experiences and problems. No attempt is made to give the full sweep of history of Old Testament times.

Specifically, the purpose of the course is to help juniors:

(1) identify themselves with seven characters to whom God revealed himself as they as juniors live imaginatively in the experiences of these persons;

(2) appreciate the Bible as a unique resource for knowing God and his will for people;

(3) grow in their own understanding and relationship to God.

DEVELOPMENT OF THE COURSE

The unit utilizes the interest of junior age boys and girls in people, especially persons who perform outstanding deeds. The characters studied will be of special interest because they helped to make God known. Effort has been made to emphasize the dramatic events in the lives of the seven chosen characters.

Juniors have had previous study of the Bible and have been introduced to some, if not all, of the "men who dared" in this course. Early in the unit a test is given to discover what they already know. A test in the form of a class-made quiz is given frequently to help boys and girls consciously add to their knowledge of Bible facts.

As boys and girls learn how God dealt with chosen leaders, they will have questions about their own relationship to God.

7

The unit provides for study and consultation to answer those questions. Comparisons of leaders of ancient times and leaders of today will also answer many questions.

Research activities, Bible reading, worship through biblical selections, reliving certain Old Testament experiences, will enrich the course and help juniors identify with the seven characters chosen by God to do his work.

Plans for ten sessions are outlined and suggestions made for several kinds of adaptations. This is to give teachers opportunities to key their teaching to individual differences and demands of their groups. Any one session may be enlarged upon or omitted as fits the situation.

JUNIORS

In vacation school juniors are usually those who have finished fourth, fifth, and sixth grades. Some schools will have low junior departments made up of third and fourth graders, and high junior departments with fifth and sixth graders. Whatever the grade grouping, children from nine to eleven display similar characteristics. They are purposeful and curious, willing to work hard for results. They take pride in work well done and can appreciate each other's contributions. They recognize good leaders and follow co-operatively. Therefore teachers need plenty of background and good preparation.

Many juniors are good readers and can handle Bible atlases, the Bible, news magazines, and maps. There will be slow readers who need help from advanced pupils. Opportunities for advanced pupils to 'teach' should occur regularly as an accepted procedure. Younger juniors sometimes write laboriously. They often draw better than they write. A number of ways of expression should be open to them. A way to help slow learners is to give them places on committees where they can work with those with quicker responses. Such plans are included in the text.

PREPARATION OF TEACHERS

It goes without saying the teachers must prepare ahead of time and daily after the sessions begin. This course is planned so that one teacher can take care of a class of eight or ten. When the number goes beyond that, two or more assistants are needed. All planning should be done co-operatively.

Teachers should practice any and all activities suggested for pupils to do. Time should be scheduled for teachers to practice activities, sing the suggested songs, write litanies, lead in worship.

Teachers must prepare to understand boys and girls. First of all they must be ready to listen and to sense when a pupil is ready to question or comment. Spending time with individual children is part of the task. Expressing friendliness is all-important.

THE USE OF THE BIBLE

The Bible is constantly in use in this unit. Each session makes use of specific selections that need to be studied and used for background, enrichment, worship material, information, enjoyment. The stories are Bible stories. The charts at the beginning of the unit present a summary of Bible references used. One purpose of the course is to help boys and girls interpret Bible passages for their own help and enlightenment.

WORSHIP

Worship should be one of the high points in each session. In a course such as this where juniors are learning how God chose and directed the lives of others, a consciousness of God's presence and direction for them should be a part of worship. Worship is shutting out the world and opening the heart to the conscious presence of God so that his guidance and help may enter into the life of those who are seeking to respond to his constant awareness of and concern for them.

If this is so, we must recognize that adult leadership in worship is almost essential. Juniors may have a part, but only when and where such leadership by juniors will truly lead the group to worship and not be a hindrance or distraction by reason of inexperience and ineptness. Training in leadership for worship may be part of the worship committee activities each day. It will probably be wise for the teachers, as they plan for several days or a week, to think about what the outcome in worship may be for their group. Then one teacher may be responsible for working with the junior committee in whatever parts are to be undertaken by them. In any case, the junior committee should change every two or three days. One teacher had a committee of four, with one member going off and a new one coming on each day, thus giving continuity, but also gradually having the entire committee new, with rotating membership. See the section on worship on pp. 123-126 for specific helps.

Junior Committees

Juniors work best in short-time assignments. For this reason it is wise to change personnel of committees every two or three days. If continuity is desired (and sometimes a complete change is better), it can be achieved by dropping the person who has been on longest and adding a new one each day. Committees should be allowed to do real planning, so far as possible. The teacher who is helping needs, however, to know how things can be done, what is within reach of her particular group's ability or circumstances, and what materials are available or can be obtained. Sometimes a brand-new suggestion by a committee proves to be feasible and well worth taking up. One teacher who was putting on a play and had no plan for costumes, was delighted when one small girl remarked, "I just love to make myself gorgeous!" The problem of costumes was solved for that group.

PICTURES

Besides illustrated reference books and maps, the junior department will need other pictures and possibly a filmstrip or two. Pictures of life in Old Testament times can be selected from the *Picture Sets for Group and Closely Graded Series.* A paperbound picture atlas might be taken apart and some of the photographs mounted for easy handling. Teachers should study the illustrations in the pupil's book and be prepared to use them for reference. It would be an interesting contrast to mount and display colored travel posters of Israel today. Enlarged pictures of any or all of the seven Bible characters will stimulate discussion (see the picture of David in the Activity Packet).

Numerous filmstrips and sound filmstrips are available to help make vivid the lives of the characters studied. The latest editions of the Audio-Visual catalogue from your denominational publisher should be consulted. There are available, a 26-frame filmstrip on Abraham, a whole series on Moses, a 36-frame filmstrip on Amos, Shepherd of Tekoa, one of David, the Shepherd Boy, with a script suggesting activities, a vivid filmstrip of Jeremiah depicting his acts of faith and comfort. Teachers would do well to order a few of the filmstrips described in their catalogue and preview them well in advance of the beginning of vacation church school.

It often happens that a member of a community has traveled in Bible lands and has colored slides that he will show on request. Juniors could plan a program when the slides would be shown and they could exhibit their projects for their parents.

THE DAILY SCHEDULE

Set up a tentative time schedule. Printed below is a possible one for the procedures suggested, but you should really work out your own. In any case the schedule should not be too rigid. You may want, when actually carrying out the session, to give twice as much time to a selected activity and omit other things, so mark those that may take more time, and those which can be done with less time or even omitted.

 9:30 Registration and activities that will accompany it
10:00 Learning names
10:10 Introducing the course
10:20 Quiz
10:35 Introduction to story; story; discussion
10:55 Research
11:15 Games
11:30 Work time
12:00 Clearing up
12:05 Worship
12:15 Closing

You may have three hours. Expand what will be enriched by more time. You may have only two hours. Shorten procedures or take fewer procedures and let such things as research and work be divided among the pupils rather than having each undertake an entire procedure.

THE PUPIL'S BOOK

The pupil's book, also entitled, *Men Who Dared in Bible Times,* contains brief stories, guidance for Bible study, poems, prayers, songs, Bible verses. It is beautifully illustrated by Esther Bell. Each pupil should have a book to take home. Copies should be on hand also for classroom use.

THE ACTIVITY PACKET

An Activity Packet of ten work sheets and an Instruction Sheet is available. Suggestions for use are worked into session plans. The Packets are not essential but are useful, particularly to schools who do not have an abundance of supplies. If the Packets are to be used, each pupil should have one.

RESOURCES

BASIC SUPPLIES

Pencils, crayons, chalk, water-color or poster paints, and brushes. Paper: typewriter-size paper, large sheets of wrapping paper, tough grocery-bag paper, construction paper in varied shades, newspapers, odds and ends of wallpaper, blackboard or large sheets of paper thumbtacked to a piece of plywood and put on an easel so used sheets can be flipped over.

Pins, scissors, needles, thread, paste, brushes, erasers, clips, masking tape, clip clothespins, string and twine, yarn.

Containers, such as wide-mouthed bottles, small and large cartons, bowls to hold water, flower vases, tin cans.

Bibles, hymnbooks, song books, game books, background books and magazines for the juniors.

Washcloths, soap, towels, rags, paper towels, paper napkins, plastic sponge.

First aid kit.

Odds and ends of materials for costumes, either large for personal use, or small for making puppets, or both.

Tear sheets of pictures of all sorts from magazines.

Books for Teachers

These Are Your Children, Gladys Jenkins, Helen Shacter and W. W. Bauer (revised), Scott, Foresmen & Co.

The Spiritual Growth of Children, Dorothy B. Fritz, Westminster Press

Teaching Juniors, Faye DeBeck Flynt, Judson Press

Working with Juniors at Church, Dorothy La Croix Hill, Abingdon Press

The Storyteller in Religious Education, Jeanette Perkins Brown, Pilgrim Press

More Children's Worship in the Church School, Jeanette Perkins Brown, Harper and Brothers

Here's How and When, Armilda B. Keiser, Friendship Press

Let's Play a Story, Elizabeth Allstrom, Friendship Press

Activities in Child Education, Elizabeth M. Lobingier, Pilgrim Press

Games for Boys and Girls, E. O. Harbin, Abingdon Press

Hymns for Junior Worship, Westminster Press

Singing Worship, Edith Lovell Thomas, Abingdon Press

The Whole World Singing, Edith Lovell Thomas, Friendship Press

Biblical Archaeology, G. Ernest Wright, Westminster Press

Light from the Ancient Past, Jack Finegan, Princeton University Press

Shorter Atlas of the Bible, Luc. H. Grollenberg, Thomas Nelson & Sons

The Westminster Historical Atlas to the Bible, G. E. Wright and Floyd B. Filson, Westminster Press

Harper's Bible Dictionary, Madeleine S. and J. Lane Miller, Harper and Brothers

The Bible Today, (by Biblical Scholars), Harper & Brothers

Understanding the Old Testament, Bernhard W. Anderson, Prentice-Hall, Inc.

The Living Story of the New Testament, Walter B. Bowie, Prentice-Hall, Inc.

An Introduction to the New Testament, Edgar J. Goodspeed, University of Chicago Press

Articles in *National Geographic Magazine:*

"We Dwelt in Kashgai Tents," June, 1952

"Pilgrims Follow the Christmas Star," December, 1952

"Bringing Old Testament Times to Life," December, 1957

"Jerusalem, the Divided City," April, 1959

"The Last Thousand Years Before Christ," December, 1960

Books for Boys and Girls

The Golden Bible Atlas, Samuel Terrien, Golden Press

Bible Stories, Mary Alice Jones, Rand McNally Co.

Cave of Riches: The Story of the Dead Sea Scrolls, Alan Honour, McGraw-Hill Book Co.

Junior Bible Archeology, Harold Victor Morsley, The Macmillan Co.

Rand McNally Historical Atlas of the Holy Land, Rand McNally Co.

The Graphic Bible, Lewis Browne, The Macmillan Co.

Picture Story of the Middle East, Susan R. Nevil, David McKay Co.

Bible Readings for Boys and Girls, Thomas Nelson & Sons

Bible Dictionary for Boys and Girls, Manuel and Odette Komroff, John C. Winston Co.

Perilous Voyage, Elsie Ball, Abingdon Press

First to Be Called Christians, Ethel L. Smither, Abingdon Press

The Bible Story for Boys and Girls—Old Testament, Walter R. Bowie, Abingdon Press

The Bible Story for Boys and Girls—New Testament, Walter R. Bowie, Abingdon-Cokesbury Press

Moses: Egyptian Prince, Law-giver, John W. Flight, Beacon Press

A Picture Dictionary of the Bible, Ruth P. Tubby, Abingdon Press

SESSION AND PURPOSE	BIBLE MATERIAL	ACTIVITIES
1. WILL MY PEOPLE DARE? To introduce the study; to guide juniors in learning how God called Abraham to venture into unknown territory to found the nation that would be faithful, and through whom God could bring blessing to the world. To guide boys and girls to desire to lend themselves to God's guidance toward his purpose for their own lives.	*Genesis* 11:31; 12:1-4; 12:5-9; 12:10; 13:1-4; 13:5-13; 13:14-18; 21:1-3, 8; 23:1-20, 24; 25:7-11; (Stories of Abraham) *Hebrews* 11:8-19	Arrival (registration and getting-acquainted games) Class activities: What's ahead A quiz Story: "From the Land of the Two Rivers" Research activities: 1. Studying a map of Bible lands 2. Reading articles and looking at pictures of "diggings" 3. Finding out all about Abraham (from the Bible) 4. Listing dates for a time line 5. Learning ideas about God in Abraham's day Reports from the researchers Planning work and choosing Recreation activities Having fun with work 1. Making clay tablets 2. Making tent-life scenes 3. Making time line: Abraham, Isaac, Jacob, Joseph 4. Making a worship book: writing a prayer 5. Learning a hymn, "With Happy Voices Ringing" 6. Beginning "I am Abraham" 7. Making out quiz questions 8. Preparing letter to parents Worship Closing time
2. I WILL RAISE UP A LEADER To continue the study with the story of Moses' early life and to help the juniors to find out more about how God challenges people to love and serve him; to encourage boys and girls to want to make themselves fit to serve God wherever they are.	*Exodus* 1:1—2:10; 2:11—3:1; 3:1—4:17; 12:30-39; 16:1-3, 35; 25:1-9; 31:1-11; 39:32, 42-43 *Deuteronomy* 5:1—6:9 (Stories of Moses and his people)	Early arrivals: Get ready for the session Games and worship committees plan Class activities: Quiz time Working on time line: Abraham to Moses Study: "God's Plan for Moses" Playing out scenes from Moses' life: 1. His rescue by the princess 2. His attempt to stop the quarrel 3. Jethro's daughters 4. Alone in the wilderness Continuing research on: 1. Map of Bible lands 2. Archeology of Bible Lands 3. The gods of Egypt, Babylonia, or Canaan 4. Nomad life

15

SESSION AND PURPOSE	BIBLE MATERIAL	ACTIVITIES
		5. Other research begun in Session 1 **Recreation: (See pages 121 to 123)** Having fun with work Worship (as planned by adult leader and committee) Closing time
3. GO DOWN, MOSES To acquaint juniors with experiences of Moses as he finally accepts God's purpose for his life and with God's help becomes the great lawgiver and leader of God's people; to guide the juniors to see how under God, people can accomplish for his great purposes what they could not otherwise do, and to encourage them to desire God's guidance in their lives.	*Exodus* 3:2—40:36 (for background) Specifically: (in order of use) *Exodus* 18:6, 12, 13-27; 32:1-6, 15-20; 25:1-9; 22: 25—23:12; 20: 1-17; 35:30—36: 5 *Deuteronomy* 4:15-24; 6:4-9; 7:6-9; 8:8-20	Early arrivals: Work on games, worship, special committees Look at work begun and continuing with it Prepare costumes for dramatizations Class activities: Adding to worship books Quiz time Dramatizations from last session Story: "Moses Faces the Pharaoh!" Research into Moses' work in the wilderness Reports on research Recreation as planned by committee Having fun with work Worship (using scripture and songs from the course) Closing time
4. HE SHALL SING OF ME TO MY PEOPLE To guide the juniors to see David as a lad and man so atune to God's will that God would be able to call him to a great task and find him responsive to guidance; to help the juniors feel that they, too, can listen to God's word as they grow toward greater knowledge of God, and prepare to do God's will.	*1 Samuel* 16:1—31: 8 Specifically: (in order of use) *1 Samuel* 16:1-13, 14-23; 18:1-9, 12-16; 10:8-10, 18; 20:1-11, 24-42; 22:1-2; 23:1-5; 24; 31:1-2, 8	Early arrivals: Work on games, exhibit, and worship committees Look at pictures and story books about David Class activities: Quiz time Work on choral reading Story: "David and King Saul" Research: shepherd life in Israel David's life (from the Bible) Reports on research Recreation Having fun with work 1. Continuing with the exhibit: shepherd life 2. Choral reading 3. Memory work 4. Adding to the quiz questions 5. Continuing "I am . . ." 6. Planning a dramatization about David 7. Something special for tomorrow **Worship (as planned by the committee)** Closing time

16

SESSION AND PURPOSE	BIBLE MATERIAL	ACTIVITIES

5. YOUR POWER SHALL LEAD MY PEOPLE
 	
To help juniors know David better, seeing how he lent himself to God's guidance, repenting and seeking forgiveness when he sinned, leading his people in worship of God, making his tribespeople into a nation; to help the juniors want to lend themselves more fully to God's guidance in their lives.
	2 Samuel (for background)
	Specifically:
	2 Samuel 1:1-12; 2: 1-7; 5:1-5, 9-12, 17-25; 6:12-15, 17-19; 7:1-17, 18-29; 8:15; 9:1-7; 11:14-15, 17, 26; 12:1-10, 13; 22:1-4, 17-26; 23:1-4; 24:18-25
		Early arrivals:
		    Work on games, exhibit, worship, and special event committees. Finish up various activities
		Class activities:
		    Quiz time
		    Dramatization of scenes in David's life
		    Story: "David the King and Leader"
		    Discussion of David as a king true to his God
		Recreation (perhaps a picnic or hike planned last session)
		Having fun with work
		    1. Selecting and learning Scripture passages
		    2. Adding to exhibits
		    3. Further work on dramatization
		    4. Continuing "I am . . ."
		    5. "Putting away" for the weekend
		    6. Plans for sharing with others on Sunday
		Worship: "God's Love and Power in Our Lives"
		Closing time.

6. GO TO BETHEL!
 	
To help boys and girls learn that Amos, a simple shepherd, called by God and obedient to him, became a powerful witness for righteousness; to guide juniors in observing that those who worshiped God by words only failed to receive his blessing.
	Book of Amos (as background)
	Specifically:
	Amos 1:1-5, 6, 9, 11, 13; 2:1, 4-8; 3:1-15; 5:8-9, 16-17, 21-24; 7:10-15; 8:4-7
		Early arrivals:
		    Get ready for the session by getting out materials, choosing pictures, arranging room. Games and worship committees work
		Class study: Review of last five sessions
		    Quiz time with panel of leaders
		    Introduction to story
		    Story: "Only a Herdsman"
		    Dramatic reading of the story of Amos
		    Evaluation and planning time
		Recreation
		Recall: "God's Purpose and Man's Response"
		Having fun with work:
		    1. The exhibit: diorama, or poster picture or frieze of Amos' story; "I am . . ." preparation
		    2. Memory work: What Amos said
		        Time line additions
		    3. Quiz questions
		Worship: "Seek Good and Not Evil"
		Closing time

SESSION AND PURPOSE	BIBLE MATERIAL	ACTIVITIES

7. YOU SHALL NOT FEAR
To help the juniors gain some knowledge of Jeremiah and the work that God did through him, and an appreciation of the devotion and courage that may be needed to carry forward God's work in the world.
	Book of Jeremiah (for background)
	Specifically: (in order of use)
	Jeremiah 1:6-9; 32: 1-5; 36:1-4, 5-7, 9-10, 14*b*-19, 20-23, 24-32; 29:1-3, 5-14; 43:4-7; 44:1
		Early arrivals:
		  Get ready for the session by games and worship committees
		  Get the quiz ready
		Class activities:
		  Singing or learning a new song
		  Quiz time
		  Introduction to the story
		  Story: "Jeremiah and God's Message"
		  Discussion of giving project
		Games or other recreation
		Planning for the next three days
		Having fun with work:
		  1. Making pictures for the time line
		  2. The exhibit: diorama, poster or drawings to illustrate Jeremiah's story
		  3. Dramatizing interview with Jeremiah or filmstrip on Jeremiah
		Worship: "The Bible Is God's Word to Us"
		Closing time

8. FIRM AS A ROCK
To guide the juniors to realize how the power of God through Jesus Christ and the Holy Spirit, entered into Peter's life and changed him to one whom God could use as a powerful witness.
	The Gospels and parts of the Book of Acts (as background)
	Specifically: (in order of use)
	Mark 1:16, 18; 9:2-8
	Matthew 16: 13-20
	John 13:36-38; 18: 25-27; 21:15-27
	Luke 22:59-62
	Acts 2:14, 22-24, 32; 3:1-15; 4:1-5, 5-13, 19-20; 5:40-42; 10; 15: 6-11
		Early arrivals:
		  Sing, browse, finish up, prepare parts for today's session
		Class activities:
		  Quiz time
		  Introduction to the story
		  Story: "Firm as a Rock"
		  Committee reports on plans for the final session
		Recreation
		Having fun with work
		  1. Frieze of Peter's life
		  2. Time line addition
		  3. Exhibit of completed projects
		  4. Dramatics (puppets, live shows, interviews)
		  5. Bible study
		  6. Making a scroll with Peter's quotation from the Psalms
		Worship: "God's Love for the World"
		Closing time

9. NOT YOUR WAY BUT MY WAY
To guide the juniors to know and admire Paul as one whom God chose to carry the gospel message near and far in the Greek and Roman world, and
	Book of Acts; Pauline epistles (for background)
	Specifically:
	Acts 7:58—8:1; 9: 1-30; 16:11-40; 17:16-18; 19:21 —20:1; 27:1—28:10
		Early arrivals:
		  Get ready for the session in worship, games, and last day committees
		  Sing and browse through books, maps, and completed projects
		Class activities:
		  Quiz time
		  Introduction to Paul

SESSION AND PURPOSE	BIBLE MATERIAL	ACTIVITIES

as one who gave with unswerving devotion all that he had; to help the juniors to gain in their desire to give their lives in support of the great cause of Christ in the church.	*Philippians* 4:8; *Colossians* 3:20, 23; *1 Thessalonians* 5:12-18, 21-22; *1 Corinthians* 10:23-24; *Romans* 12:9-18; *Hebrews* 12:2-14	Story: "The Story of Paul"
		 Recall of previous sessions and evaluation
		 Bible study: Paul's message
		 Recreation
		 Plans for next session (This will include planning how to share with parents)
		 Having fun with work:
		   1. Completing the time line
		   2. Making a litany
		   3. Working on the exhibit
		   4. Dramatization (puppets, live, interview, letter from Paul)
		   5. Rehearsal for the last session
		   6. Conversation and summary
		 Worship: "God and His World"
		 Closing time

10. The KINGDOM SHALL BECOME
 To guide the juniors to gather together the threads of the study and think further about what God's purpose demands in our lives today; to recall main events in the lives of men who dared as they carried out God's purposes.
	Selections from scriptures used in the course	**Plan 1**
		 Early arrivals:
		   Get ready for the session by arranging the room, working on exhibit and other committees, preparing for guests
		 Class activities:
		   Written quiz
		   Recall
		   Program for the guests, including:
		   Worship: "Giving Praise to God"
		 Recreation in which the guests join, viewing filmstrip, and slides on Bible Lands
		 Getting ready to take things home
		 Dismissal
		 Plan II
		 Early arrivals:
		   Arrange the room, work on committees, review pupil's book, study the Bible using references
		 Class activites:
		   Recall planned by the juniors
		   Recreation
		   A program for ourselves
		   Conducted tour of the exhibit
		   Worship: "Giving Praise to God"
		   Getting ready to take things home
		 Dismissal

Will My People Dare?

The Whole Study is about people of the Bible whom God called to serve him in special ways and through whose growing loyalty, devotion, and courage he was able to reveal himself more fully to the world.

We Begin with the story of Abraham, who because of his confidence and faith in God, was willing to venture into unknown territory and to endure the difficulties and hardships of establishing a new home for the people of God.

The Story of God's choice of Abraham and of Abraham's response to God's purpose for his life is found in Genesis 11:25—25:10 and in Hebrews 11:8-19; with the following references used particularly in this session: Genesis 11:31; 12:1-4; 12:5-9; 12:10; 13:1-4; 13:5-13; 13:14-18; 21:1-3, 8; 23:1-20; 24; 25:7-11.

The Juniors should be drawn to Abraham through this day's study. At the close of the session they should have an increased desire to lend themselves to God's guidance, and a greater willingness to have a part in carrying out God's great purpose for mankind in their own lives.

HIGHLIGHTS FOR THE FIRST SESSION

Arrival (registration and getting-acquainted games)

Class Activities:

What's Ahead? (the introduction of the course to the juniors)

A Quiz (to find out what boys and girls already know about the Bible background)

Story: "From the Land of the Two Rivers"

Research Activities:
1. Studying a map of Bible lands
2. Reading articles and looking at pictures of "diggings"
3. Finding out all about Abraham (from the Bible)
4. Listing dates for a time line
5. Learning ideas about gods in Abraham's day

Reports from the Researchers
Planning Work and Choosing Activities
Recreation
Having Fun With Work
1. Clay tablets: I AM YOUR GOD AND YOU ARE MY PEOPLE
2. Tent-life scenes
3. Time line: Abraham, Isaac, Jacob, Joseph
4. Worship book: Writing a prayer
5. Learning a hymn
6. Beginning "I am Abraham"
7. Making out quiz questions
8. Preparing letter to parents

Worship
Closing Time

GETTING READY FOR THE FIRST DAY

Read The Session. Following it you will find a section on how to plan your very own session using these suggestions but adapting them to your needs. You will find help in how to make your own notebook for this course.

THE SESSION

As the Juniors Come

You look up from wherever you are and see someone with a turned-up nose and a freckled face standing in the doorway. A tinge of excitement runs through you. Here begins an adventure—the meeting of mind with mind—and who knows to what it will lead? You reach toward it with face beaming.

The child is a stranger. Your welcome makes him feel wanted and secure. It is a factor in his coming again.

Or he is already known to you and a new, richer relationship is to be achieved.

21

Each child as he comes in gets a warm, personal greeting and is helped to occupy himself.

Registration

Registration proceeds according to plan. (See page 120, Appendix.) An activity easily dropped or taken up again by individual children should occupy those not being registered at the moment so that no idle crowd is waiting for a turn to register or for something to start after being enrolled.

You will choose one of the following activities or a similar one. If registration takes a long time you must be ready with a second activity. Whatever it is must be *fun*.

Making and decorating huge name tags (page 120).

Preparing and mailing a letter to parents (pages 29 and 120).

Experimenting with puppets.

Playing a quiet competitive game with two sides (page 121). Two children at a time may go to be registered and two at a time return to the game, thus keeping the sides even. A helper or the lead teacher should conduct each activity.

Learning Names

You have already decided how much time is needed for this. (See Planning for the First Session, page 31.) The name tags are needed *if only one child or helper* does not know everyone else. In any case, play a name-using game at least once. If a fair number of those present are strangers to each other, break into a name-learning game several times during the session even though no place for it is indicated on these pages.

What's Ahead?

The boys and girls will gather for their introduction to the study ahead of them. You may say something of this sort: "Vacation church school is a wonderful time. It is wonderful because we have *time*. Time to do what? What have you enjoyed most in vacation church school in other years?" (List the answers the juniors give on a chalkboard, for they will give you a clue to what has had so much interest or worth *that it was remembered*. If they do not mention *thinking about important things* and *learning to know more about God*, you many suggest them.) "We are going to do most of these things and some others besides."

You may go on to say: "In the Bible we find the marvelous story of how God has worked, down through all the years, to bring mankind to a loving, loyal devotion to himself. Because he is our Father, and loves us, he gives us a share in his work. Sometimes what God asks us to do seems impossible. It takes great courage, or great devotion, or great faith, or just simple great determination."

You may ask: "Have you ever wondered how God was able to begin with just one family, Abraham's, and to develop from it a great nation who loved him and wanted to do his will? In our study this next few days we will come to know more about how God chose certain men who were to help him carry out his wonderful purpose for mankind because they were willing to follow his guidance and receive his help. We will find them daring to do things that astonish us. Most of us might not have the courage and devotion and determination that they showed. The stories of these men are in the Bible.

"They dared to do what they attempted because in a way God said to them, I have an impossible job to be done, and you are the person I want to do it. Will you? I will go with you and guide you and help you if you are willing to undertake this task."

You may then ask the juniors, "Would you like to guess which people in the Bible are the ones we will be thinking about? Which ones do you think they may be?"

Boys and girls familiar with the Bible will have suggestions. They may mention some of the seven we are to study (Abraham, Moses, David, Amos, Jeremiah, Peter, Paul) and they may mention others. You may list them all and underline those listed above.

You might conclude: "We'll need to find out what it was God wanted these men to do, and why it was difficult, and whether they really showed love and devotion in doing it. Their stories are full of excitement."

A Quiz

Everyone loves a quiz. Give each boy and girl the quiz sheet from his Activity Packet. (Sheet No. 2, "For the Beginning of the Study.")

If you are using the Activity Sheets explain that after the name of each person about whom we plan to study, there are various statements. Only one of those statements is correct. Each pupil is to try to remember what he knows about that person and find the correct statement and underline it. Suggest that he leave it unmarked unless he knows or feels pretty sure he knows. Tell the pupils that they will have another chance at the test at the end of the unit. Ask each to put his name at the top. Then give time for the underlining. (If the juniors have been seated quite close together, scatter them before they start underlining.) In some situations you may want to let each choose a partner to work with *before* you give out the sheets. When all have finished, gather up the sheets. Be sure that the name is on each. Or you may let each correct his own sheet.

Introduction to the Story

Many years ago, when people read the story of Abraham, they noticed that the Bible said he came from Ur, a city of the Chaldees. Some people were very scornful. They said, "There is no such city." Or they said, "There never was such a city." It was true that nowhere in all the Bible lands could any trace be found of such a city.

But in the nineteenth century, there was a man who believed that Ur and other ancient cities did exist. He thought they might be buried under great mounds of sand. So he went to the land where the Chaldeans lived. He found a huge earth and sand mound. Wandering tribespeople said there was a city buried underneath it. The explorer hired diggers who began to shift the earth and sand.

Sure enough! Under great mounds of dust and sand and decay, the excavator found the very city from which Abraham set out, the city of Ur of the Chaldees. He found many very strange and wonderful things there, and he found out a great deal about the gods whom the people of that ancient city worshiped and about the customs of that day and age.

Story: "From the Land of the Two Rivers"

(Use the story as given in the pupil's book.)

Discussion:

The juniors may consider such questions as: Why did God want Abraham and his family to go away from the cities and into a rural land? (The cities were devoted to worship of many gods. Country life would make it easier to follow God's leading.) Why did God choose Canaan? (It was a fertile land between two great

24

areas of civilization. It was a land with space where a new people could live. It was a small area where a family could grow to be a nation with laws and customs.) Why was it hard for Abraham? (Nomadic life in a new land is always hard.) Why did it take faith? (Because Abraham was getting old and had no children. Yet God's promise was that in his descendants all the world should be blessed.) How did Abraham show that he was devoted to God? (At every major camp he set up a stone altar for the worship of God.) How was this different from the worship of the people around? (Abraham did not worship an image of a god. God demanded righteousness from Abraham and his family and his workers.)

Time to Look at Materials and Get Ideas

Have the assistant teachers and other helpers at the tables or bookshelves where you have displayed the reference books and maps that will be needed in the course. Let the pupils now examine the materials and ask questions. Have slips of paper in books to mark sections on Abraham, "diggings" in Ur, patriarchs, nomad life, worship in Babylonia or Canaan, or other subjects that will stimulate ideas for research. Encourage pupils to sit down and read, or study a map with a partner. Allow about 10 minutes for this. Then call the group together. Talk about what the boys and girls have found out.

Research Plans

Write on the chalkboard or on a large sheet of paper, the items, one under the other, on which research may be done. The ones to be suggested are: Map; Diggings; All About Abraham; Starting a Time Line; Ideas About Gods in Abraham's Day. You may not have materials for some of the activities. If so, omit them. There may be other areas for which you do have materials. Include them. You may have just a few juniors and want to let them pick out just a couple of areas for research. The map, "About Abraham," and the time line may be the ones chosen by the juniors.

Either divide by appointing leaders and having them choose teams, or assign the children, or let each junior choose what he wishes to do.

25

1. Map Work. Find the places of Abraham's journeys. Ur, Haran, Canaan, Egypt, Shechem, Bethel, Hebron are marked on the map on Sheet No. 3 in the Activity Packet. A Bible atlas, if you have a good one, will give these and other points, such as The Negeb, and Mamre. Limited research will simply take the story as given in the pupil's book, and find the places mentioned there. Since this map will be used throughout the study, this group may want to work at enlarging it to make a map sixteen times as big, which would be about 39 inches by 54 inches. Four spaces the exact size of the map in the packet both vertically and horizontally, will give the measurements and if lightly ruled will give a guide for enlarging. See Activity Sheet No. 4 for directions for enlarging maps and pictures.

2. Diggings (or to put it more technically, archeology). Whether or not you have this activity will depend on your resources. The juniors will want to look up Ur in a Bible atlas, such as the *Golden Bible Atlas.* Discovery of that city with its light on religion, common names, and customs has helped us know more about Abraham's day. The juniors may read about this ancient city, perhaps finding out about its excavation, and looking at pictures of the amazing things found there. They should prepare to tell about a few of the things they find out. Teachers should find and insert slips of paper to indicate references in such books as *The Golden Bible Atlas; Rand McNally Historical Atlas of the Holy Land; The Graphic Bible,* by Lewis Browne; *The Westminster Historical Atlas to the Bible.*

3. All About Abraham. This is Bible study. The juniors may check the following references: Genesis 11:31; 12:1-4; 12:5-9; 12:10; 13:1-4; about Lot's choice 13:5-13; about God's promise to Abraham, 13:14-18; the birth of Isaac, 21:1-3, 8; the buying of a burial place, 23:1-20; choosing a wife for Isaac, chapter 24; Abraham's death, 25:7-11. You may instead have a Bible story-book that gives Abraham's story in brief, and let the juniors pick out some incidents from it for telling.

4. Ideas About Gods in Abraham's Day. Refer to Bible dictionaries and atlases for information about worship in those early days. The juniors may look at them and get an idea of the many gods that the peoples worshiped. They may also learn that the gods worshiped then did not, in people's minds, demand goodness, or truth, or any of the values that we find in God's demands

on his people. They may find something about the sacrifices—often human sacrifices—that were made to these gods. Teachers should examine and insert markers at the page references in the books or magazines available.

5. Finding Out About Tent Life. While this is not in the session plans until later, you may prefer to start it now instead of some of the new ideas above. Church school units for grades 5 and 6 often have background for such study in Old Testament history. Investigate what is used in your Sunday church school and bring the units for reference.

Reports on Progress

If desired, some time may be taken to report on progress of each activity before rest time.

Recreation

Teachers may have planned recreation for this session. It may consist of active or quiet games, or a brief hike to get out of doors and change the atmosphere. See suggestions for games on page 122.

Planning Further Work and Choosing Activities

As the juniors come to this time, they may be helped to see that there are many ways of undertaking creative activities. One boy or girl may want to work at something alone. Later others may want to join in. But once a thing is undertaken it should be finished. You may illustrate: "Each of you may want to make your worship book [show your sample]. Or, some two or three who like to cut and paste may enjoy getting all the worship books ready. Or part of you may want to do that and the rest something else. As a rule it is a good idea to finish what we begin so that we don't have a great many unfinished things left lying around."

Then ask for choices to be made, beginning with what you think the most important to get done. It will save "Oh! I'd have chosen that!" from disappointed children, if you list everything you plan to propose where all can see the list.

Work tables, a clean floor, an outdoor nook, chairs to work on, should be ready with materials set out.

1. *Making clay tablets.* See directions on Sheet number 4 from the Activity Packet, or use directions from how-to-do-it books.

2. *Setting up a shepherd scene.* See "Scenes" on Activity Sheet Number 8, or use ideas from other sources.

3. Adding to *time line.* See Activity Sheet Number 5, or make up your own time-line suggestions.

4. Adding to *worship books.* Sheet No. 6 of the Activity Packet provides some material for the worship books. Selections are to be mounted on booklets made by folding typewriter paper in four. Two sheets will make a 16-page booklet. (The top of the fold must be cut on the first folding.) The Activity Sheet is to be cut along the solid lines and folded on the dotted lines accordion fashion, after the lower half of the sheet is pasted to the upper half as indicated. Now slip the accordion-folded sections *over* the pages in the booklet. The title page will cover page 1 of the booklet with the folded edge of the activity sheet fold to the right, the fold of the booklet to the left. This will bring the second piece of the accordion-folded material over page 2, the third piece over page 3. See diagram on the instruction sheet. (If you do not have the Activity Sheets, you may prefer to use charts of songs and prayers of your own devising.)

Some pages are left blank for the juniors to create their own prayers and to put in other materials of their own choice. Children may want to write an opening prayer, or a closing prayer of thanks for a happy day, during this work period.

5. *Learning a Hymn.* See page 127.

6. *Beginning Impersonations.* Stories of seven men are found in this study. The juniors may enjoy preparing statements which each character might give if he were present and wished to tell briefly about his life. If you have puppets, or are going to make them, the boys and girls will enjoy costuming them appropriately and having them "give" the speeches. The speeches should be very much in the juniors' own words and be as lively as they can make them.

Each may start, if he likes, with the words "I am" followed by the name of the person being portrayed. "I am Abraham. I was born in a city called Ur. When I was grown up, my father took our family to a new land, a land far up the river of the Euphrates. Its name was Haran," and so forth. Pupils may put in any details they wish but the paragraph should not be too long. This procedure may be followed with each major person of the study if

28

the boys and girls enjoy doing it. Two or three juniors could do this, the ones choosing this activity changing with each character.

7. *Making Out Quiz Questions.* A few or all the juniors may do this. If all do it, ask each junior to write down one question about Abraham that he would like to ask "the other side," if two sides were having a quiz contest. From the questions that result, one of the helpers may make up a quiz for next session, adding questions on areas omitted. If a group of two or three are doing it, they may also each make up several questions, or they may work together to think up questions, easy and hard ones, to make a quiz for next session. The questions should be limited to information gathered today.

8. *Letter to Parents.* If this was not prepared during registration period (see page 120) using Activity Sheet No. 1, you will want to have the juniors work now with whatever letter you have prepared to go to parents.

Allow time for choice of activity. Then decide on the length of the work period according to time left in your session. Teachers will, of course, assist where needed in work groups.

Discussion and Evaluation

The juniors may gather in one group and you may guide them in a conversation in which both pupils and teachers will take part. The discussion may be something like this: Now that we have thought about Abraham and the way in which he responded to God's will for his life, let us name some of the reasons why God thought of him as a chosen leader. Could Abraham have done what de did without God's help? Why not? Did others in Abraham's family have to be ready to trust God and to co-operate with Abraham? Do we have leaders today who can help us know what is God's will for us? Does God help each of us as we try to do his will? In what ways?

You might follow the conversation by asking, "What do you think we have found out today that helps us in trying to respond to God's will?" The juniors may suggest that it helps to know about others who have followed God's will, that we have learned from the Bible how God helps those who obey him, that we have felt God's purpose more surely, and so forth.

You may say, "Tomorrow we are going to think about a man who was a descendant of Abraham's. We will find out what

29

God wanted him to do, whether he was willing to do it, and if he succeeded in serving God through his devotion and loyalty."

Clearing Up

When it is almost time for worship or your next procedure, ask the boys and girls to put everything neatly in its place so that work can be resumed easily tomorrow. Give at least five minutes for this.

Worship Preparation

Five minutes should be spent in making the boys and girls familiar with the opening worship given below. Use the worship booklets if these are being made or use some other plan.

First Leader:
Thou art the LORD, thou alone;
Thou hast made heaven, the heaven of heavens;
with all their host, the earth and all that is on it;
the seas and all that is in them;
and thou preservest all of them,
and the host of heaven worships thee.
Thou art the LORD.

Second Leader:
Stand up and bless the LORD your God
from everlasting to everlasting.

Response: (by all)
"Blessed be thy glorious name
which is exalted above all blessing and praise."[1]

All: (singing to the tune "Old Hundredth")
We come, O God, to sing Thy praise,
Through all these busy, happy days.
Help us to live in harmony,
Lord, with each other and with Thee.[2]

Two adults may take the parts of First and Second Leaders on this first day. The juniors may first read and then, if they wish, learn the spoken and sung responses. If the tune "Old Hundredth" is not familiar go over it a time or two. Your hymnal may give it under "All People Who On Earth Do Dwell."

[1]Nehemiah 9:5b-7a.
[2]G. W. McGavran.

A Possible Service of Worship

Quiet Music: "Old Hundredth."

Scripture Verses: See Sheet Number 6 of the Activity Sheets, and the poetry from "Worship Preparation."

Response: See Sheet Number 6 (to be sung to Old Hundredth) and the poetry from "Worship Preparation."

Leader: The most wonderful fact in all the world is that God, who created the heavens and the earth and all that is in them, cares for people. He cares for us and is always seeking us out, to help us, to guide us, and to let us find him. Men and women, boys and girls everywhere are responding to his love and concern for them. Let us sing a hymn of response to God.

Hymn: "With Happy Voices Ringing" (see the inside back cover of the junior's book).

Prayer: One taken from the worship booklets, given in unison by all, or a short prayer by one of the leaders.

Offering Service: (See suggestions on page 126).

Hymn: (See suggestions on page 125).

The Lord's Prayer

Benediction

Closing Time

Appoint games and worship committees for the next session. You might say, "Today we have seen how God had a plan for a family who would be his people and do his will. Abraham did his part; but a strange thing was to happen. Tomorrow we'll hear about how God rescued his people in a time of very great trouble."

Let your enjoyment of this day's work with the juniors shine out in voice and eyes and smile. Let them know you are looking forward to another day with them, as you dismiss them.

PLANNING FOR THE FIRST SESSION

The more careful the planning, the easier the work.

The more careful the planning, the more enriching the course.

The more careful the planning, the more spontaneous and heartfelt the response.

The more careful the planning, the more smoothly things will run.

Who Plans?

The lead teacher has the responsibility, but the planning should be done together by all those who are to have a part in leadership. This may include several well-trained teachers; or it may be just the lead teacher with a helper or two, depending on the situation. In any case, so far as is at all possible, all should share in the planning. Even a young helper may have an idea which will enrich the course for everyone.

Sometimes, some of the responsibilities may be divided. In that case the lead teacher or someone who is an expert along one line or another may want to have individual "learning" sessions with a less experienced helper to guide her in preparation for specific responsibilities. Sometimes a resource person who cannot attend the planning sessions is to help at some particular point. If at all possible, a resource person should, in an individual conference, be helped to see the over-all purpose and scope of the study, and be told of plans to help juniors to achieve the objectives. There are always some teachers who, because they are employed or have other responsibilities during training institutes, cannot attend them. The lead teacher, in such cases, may arrange for special times in the evening when employed persons may come to hear reports from those who attended the institutes.

As those who are to work together as leaders of the children meet to plan and think and become familiar with the content of the course and with what it may mean to the boys and girls, it is usually wise to consider the abilities of each and what each really enjoys doing. Then specific responsibilities may be accepted. Do not make this too strict. This is an opportunity for teacher growth as well as for pupil growth. Each teacher, no matter how experienced or inexperienced should emerge from this school more able to carry out various techniques, more competent to lead juniors in thought-provoking discussion, skilled in seizing moments and turning them to high points in the session.

Your Friend Notebook

An invaluable friend is your notebook. It begins to have jottings from the moment you take up the books for this course and begin to look them over. For instance, just take a look this minute at "Which?" below, and write into your notebook a brief estimate of *your* situation and how you will handle it. You are at least likely to have one or two helpers not known to all the children; at most no one will know anyone else. You also jot down "Discuss with helpers the importance of every single child's knowing everyone else and of the adults knowing every child." You will also cross out in this text the two situations not applicable to your case.

Your notebook will list who is going to do what about costume materials, about name tag materials, about background on Bible times, about experimenting with making up the worship book. For instance your notebook will carry some such note as: "Lucile will experiment with Activity Sheets No. 7 and No. 8 to see how to make a shepherd scene. Warn her not to let the children see her pattern as the scenes are to be the pupils' ideas, not hers." Jot down materials needed and who is going to secure them. After experimenting, the length of time likely to be needed to do any particular thing may be added.

You will put down a rough timetable. It may be like the one that comes in this book or quite different. In any case it must have your own slant to it. That is what makes teaching exciting. "Boys and girls, imagine how this might have been done!" may start off a discussion or research which will fill ten minutes instead of two. Your time table should include such suggestions to yourself.

On a separate page your notebook should carry the list of *all* materials you will need to carry out *your* plan for this session.

Another page will show when *all* juniors are to be involved in one activity, such as listening to the story or taking part in a discussion, and when they will be working in separate groups at activities of their choice, and who will be helping each group.

Which?

? The children all know each other and know the leaders. We can plunge right in.

? There are a few children and a few leaders who are strangers to the others. We can ask for Friendly Pals for each stranger.

? The children are from various groups and churches and many do not know each other, or the leaders. We'll play a get-acquainted game.

Steps in Planning

1. Go over all the suggestions. Decide which ones fit your situation, the age of your boys and girls, the equipment you have,

your time with the juniors, and other factors.

2. Think about the purpose of this day. You will have to do this repeatedly as you plan, but take some time when you do serious thinking about God's purpose in Abraham's life. Recall, as you read the first verses of Genesis, chapter 12, that here was the beginning of God's long reaching out toward the people of Israel through whom he was to guide the world toward himself. Think of Abraham, responding to God's call with unshakable faith, leaving all that was known to him, and venturing into a land with hostile tribes. Here was Abraham, a childless man, yet obeying a command which seemed to be based on the expectation of his descendants. Think about how this man, chosen of God to begin the establishment of his people, kept his faith through all his years, setting up altars for worship at every camp place and keeping his heart open to the guidance of God in every matter. You will need to be saturated with the feeling of the high excitement of this beginning, if you are to make this more than a more factual study for your juniors.

3. Keeping this purpose in mind, work on the factual materials you plan to use, not as ends in themselves but to show how God worked and how a faithful, devoted man responded. Prepare to give the introduction to the story, the story itself, and to lead the discussion following it. Read the story of Abraham in the Bible beginning with chapter 12 of Genesis. Make all this your own, so you do not have to refer to books. Find out as much as you can about life in early Old Testament days. Consult your Bible dictionary, and your historical atlas of the Bible. Hunt up your *National Geographic* magazine articles on Bible lands, and refer to any children's books which tell about and illustrate this period. See "Resource Books," page 14.

4. Study the pupil's book (the Activity Sheets, if you are using them) and all supplementary materials you have.

5. Gather together what you will need for activities. You will find two types of materials. First, basic supplies that should be on hand every day. A list of these is boxed in on page 12. Then you will find you need specific materials depending on what you are planning to do. These will be listed or described in the sections that tell how to carry out activities. For this first day, the *special* materials will include: materials for name tags; letters to parents; resource materials for the research groups; quiz sheets

from the Activity Packets; map from the Activity Sheets and material to make one huge map; materials for making worship booklets; clay for tablets; as well as the usual supplies which will also be needed in carrying out activities.

6. Plan an attractive room for the children to enter as they arrive for the first session. Work centers, research centers, easily available work materials, book and picture suggestions, a puppet nook where workable arrangements for puppet shows can be worked out, flowers and so forth will, if set up ahead of time, encourage interest and participation in the things you have chosen to bring alive the story of the Bible.

7. Do not forget that all are working together in this. Each teacher or helper, as you plan happily together, may undertake major responsibility for one thing or another. Be sure that all have a clear idea of what the purpose is for each thing that is planned and in what way it will advance the main purposes of the day's work.

8. Experiment with whatever you have for the boys and girls to use. A new game? Try it out to be sure the leader's directions are clear. A competitive game? See how it works out. Clay tablets? Try making them yourselves. Or one may do that, while someone else works at making a worship booklet to be used as a sample, another practices with puppets, and so forth. If possible, sing together all the hymns and music to be used, especially if a song or hymn is new to the boys and girls. Practice reading in unison with a leader the opening phrases for worship. Look through the resources material. Go over the quiz so you will know the right answers. Agree on essential rules, and on whether they are to be announced, or whether the boys and girls will be guided to make them. Rules imposed on the school by situation or outside authorities are not, of course, subject to decision by either leaders or juniors.

9. As you plan, look for highlights of the session, places where you think worship will come naturally. Study the paragraphs on page 9 of the Introduction and the section on worship resources in the Appendix. Become familiar with the worship materials given in the session plan. With this guidance in mind prepare to take advantage of any possibilities for worship that occur as you teach.

I Will Raise Up a Leader

The Whole Study shows God's way of challenging people to serve him with love and devotion. As it moves forward, it will help the juniors to become acquainted with some of those whom God chose to carry out his great purposes.

We Continue our study by seeing how God prepared a man to be able to answer God's challenge—if he would.

The Story of how God caused Moses to be given the training to suit him for God's purpose, and how Moses misused his power and had to flee for his life, but remained faithful to God, will be found in Exodus 1:1—3:1. The story of how he answered God's challenge will follow in the next part of the study. Specific references for today are: Exodus 1:1—2:10; 2:11—3:1; 3:1—4:17; 12:30-39; 16:1-3, 35; Deuteronomy 5:1—6:9; Exodus 25:1-9; 31:1-11; 39:32, 42-43.

The Juniors should begin to see how God works out his purposes through those who are willing to be guided by him toward great achievements; they should be encouraged to want to become as able as possible that God may use them for like purposes.

HIGHLIGHTS FOR THE SECOND SESSION

Early Arrivals: Getting ready for the session through games and worship committee plans. Others continue work previously begun, or enjoy the resource books available on life in Egypt.

Class Activities:

Quiz time with two sections, just for fun

Working on Time Line: Abraham to Moses
Study: "God's Plan for Moses" (Would he accept it? This story ends with Moses as a shepherd hiding in Midian)
Playing Out Scenes from Moses' Life:
1. His rescue by the princess
2. His attempt to stop the quarrel

36

3. Jethro's daughters
4. Alone in the wilderness

Continuing Research on:
1. Map of Bible lands
2. Archeology of Bible lands
3. The gods of Egypt, Babylonia, or Canaan or
4. Nomad life
5. Other research begun in Session 1

Recreation (See pages 121 to 123)

Having Fun with Work

    1. From last session: Looking at clay tablets and tent-life exhibit, continuing work as needed
    2. Continuing "I am . . ." preparation
    3. Continuing hymn study
    4. Working with memory selections
    5. Making out quiz questions from new story

Worship (as planned by adult leader and committee)

Closing Time

PLANNING FOR THE SECOND DAY

While this text does separate the procedures into ten sessions, we hope that you will not need to do so. Your class may need to do further study about how God used Abraham. If so, your plan for the second day could concern itself with Abraham. Or you may be ready to find out how Moses was used of God. In that case, you will read what we call Sessions Two and Three and work out your own plan for the two days. You might even decide to give just one day to Moses and more time to David, or three days to Moses and just one to David. You are free to use this material as seems wise to you, even to leaving out one study entirely. You are not to cover a certain amount of material, but to lead juniors to see that God has a great and wonderful purpose in this world and that he calls on men and women, boys and girls, to help cause his will to be done on earth with courage, devotion, and loyalty. No one but you can judge which story is catching fire and burning bright for the juniors in your care. No one but you can decide what is the best arrangement of the procedures for you to use.

Specific help in planning this session follows the procedures.

A POSSIBLE SECOND-DAY SESSION

As the Juniors Come

A warm welcome greets every single boy and girl, not only from you but from every helper. Late registrations may need to be taken care of, new name tags written, and introductions made.

Juniors may hurry to whatever they were doing when they were most interested in last session. Newcomers may be shown what was done. Other juniors may help them get started on making their worship books, and anything else that everyone did earlier.

Two groups of juniors may meet apart from the others. The first group is the games committee whose work is outlined in "Recreation," beginning on page 121. The other group is the worship committee. It will work with the adult who is to lead worship today.

Arrival time is often a good time to enjoy learning the hymns which are given in the pupil's book and which will, without doubt, be chosen by the worship committee to use during worship. If the children especially enjoy singing, a "singing time" may be instituted during which not only hymns but good fun songs and some lovely rounds may be sung.

Remember that although the juniors help plan what is to be done, the direction of the activities is in your hands. You may find that making a delightful worship book appeals to all the juniors or most of them. That activity may be given most of the time and familiar hymns substituted for learning several new ones. New ones can always be read in unison so the thought is not lost.

Work with puppets, or maps, or something else may entrance the boys and girls. Whatever can be done enthusiastically and completed may be given longer stretches of time than the usual "bits" each day which merely string out an activity till everyone is bored with it.

Be sure to play some learning-names games till every junior and every leader can name instantly all the rest.

Fun with a Quiz

Two sides may compete as the questions the boys and girls prepared yesterday are used to recall facts about Abraham, the lands he lived in, customs, or whatever the juniors felt was worth asking questions about. Be very sure that the correct answer is given before the question is left. A good referee is needed to conduct the quiz. Make it fast and make it fun. Suggest that after part of today's study, more questions can be made up to add next time. Suggest that the juniors be thinking of both hard and easy questions to ask, and that any time when there is nothing else they should be doing, they may dictate their questions to the leading teacher or to one of the assistants.

Put up a Quiz Box (a carton with a hole cut in the top) into which questions may be dropped as they are written on slips of paper. Each teacher may encourage group formation of questions as he goes along, by at times saying, "What quiz question could we ask about that?" The questions may be about facts but should gradually include those about attitudes, beliefs, and commitments.

Conversation

"We have begun our study with the story of Abraham. But it is not just the story of Abraham that we are interested in. What we are interested in is how God had a great plan for all the people of the world and asked Abraham to help him carry out that plan. Can you tell me what it was that God asked Abraham to do?" (The juniors should be able to respond that God called Abraham to go out into a strange land and there establish a people who would be loyal and faithful to him and through whom he could bless the families of the whole earth.) "Was Abraham willing?" (The juniors should be able to affirm that he was, and that he went forth in trust and faith, being loyal to God and establishing himself with God's help in the land which God had chosen for him.) "Did Abraham's descendants just go on living there?" (Some junior may be able to tell you, with perhaps a few hints, that under Joseph, God saved the families from destruction by famine and settled them in Egypt.) "They stayed in Egypt for many, many years. But at last the time came when God was ready to lead the family that had become thousands of people, back into Canaan, the Promised Land. For that he needed a new leader. Today we are to find out how God began to prepare such a leader."

The Years Slip By

Someone may briefly indicate the time between Abraham and Moses by mentioning that Abraham was the great-grandfather, Isaac, his son, the grandfather, Jacob, son of Isaac, the father of Joseph. This brings the descendants or "children" of Jacob, also called Israel, to Egypt and under the domination of the pharaohs. Then after years of slavery came Moses.

The time line may be brought down to the time of Moses. See Activity Sheet Number 5, if you are using the sheets.

Map study may be done at the same time if you wish. The map in the Activity Packet may be used for each junior to trace the journeys of the Patriarchs till the time of slavery in Egypt. (Abraham went there once but did not stay.) If you are not using the Activity Sheets use whatever map you chose last week.

This may be the time when you want to look at pictures of Egypt and Egyptian culture, and to break into groups to study something about the Egyptian background. Use the resource books introduced last session. Or you may prefer to do this in the work time.

Introducing Moses

Abraham had followed God's leading. He had answered God's call by leaving the old familiar scenes and finding the land where God intended his people to live. There, among a people who worshiped many gods, Abraham set up altars for the worship of the one true God.

Abraham stayed there the rest of his life, wandering as shepherd people do, from one part of the land to the other.

His son Isaac and his grandson Jacob lived in that land.

But his great-grandson Joseph was sold into slavery in Egypt and was used by God to save his father and his brothers and all their families in time of trouble. Joseph became almost as great as Pharaoh, the ruler of the land.

Other pharaohs came to the throne. Joseph died, and the "children" or descendants of Jacob, who was also called Israel, were made slaves. Their life was hard. They cried to God to save them.

The years went by. The time came when God was ready to guide the Israelites (often called Hebrews) back to the Land of Promise, the land to which he had led Abraham. How was he to rescue them from the power of Egypt? How was he to weld them into a powerful people, living by his laws and worshiping him and not the gods of the people among whom they would live? God needed a leader who would be strong, wise, firm, loyal and courageous, and who would give the people God's direction for their lives.

Alternate Plans for Study

Read "Possible Steps in Planning" on page 51 and decide what you will do. You may tell the story in two parts, one each day, and let the pupils plan several dramatizations. Instead of telling the story, you may guide the boys and girls in gathering information through directed study. Then they could read the story for themselves in the pupil's book.

Finding Out About Moses

The story of Moses has in it so many little stories, complete in themselves, that it is a good one to use for study and report. In each instance, the guidance of God and his purpose working out through the phases of Moses' life should be kept in mind.

You might start by saying: "One of the greatest characters, or persons, of the Bible is Moses. For him God had a task that seemed so impossible that no one would have believed he could carry it out. But because he was willing, with God as his leader, to try to accomplish the thing God wanted done, he grew in wisdom and strength and power to carry out the will of God for his people."

Continue, "We find the story of Moses in Exodus, the second of the books of the Bible. Let's divide into ____ groups, and each take a part of the story. We'll study and come back together and see how alive we can make the story for each other."

Assign one or more of the following parts of Moses' story to each group. You may wish to assign only one part to a group, and reserve for yourself the telling of some of the parts, interspersing these with the reports from the class.

1. The birth and childhood of Moses. Exodus 1:1—2:10.

2. His training. This is one part you will want to tell. Mention briefly how he would have been trained in all the wisdom of the Egyptians, living as he did as an adopted son of the princess, and therefore regarded as Prince Moses. Yet he had lived with his own parents, he knew he was a Hebrew, and he worshiped, not the gods of the Egyptians, but the one true God.

3. How Moses became a shepherd. Exodus 2:11—3:1.

4. When God called Moses to do a difficult task. Exodus 3:1—4:17.

5. Moses before Pharaoh. You will want to tell this yourself, making it very brief. You may say that Moses did go before Pharaoh, and that God enabled him to do many signs and wonders, but that only when death touched the Egyptian homes did Pharaoh really relent and tell Moses to take the children of Israel away. Tell how, on that night of the death of the first-born, the children of Israel killed and prepared a lamb for each family and touched the doorframes of their houses with the blood to show that they were of the children of Israel. Tell that the angel of death passed over those houses and no one inside them was harmed. That was the beginning of the Passover which has been observed from that time until today by Jewish families.

6. The people leave. Exodus 12:30-39.

7. The passage of the Red Sea. You will want to tell very briefly how Pharaoh repented that he had let the slaves go, and went after them with his army to bring them back, but that Moses with his great faith in God led them safely to freedom, while Pharaoh and his army were destroyed.

8. The wilderness and laws. Exodus 16:1-3, 35; Deuteronomy 5:1—6:9.

9. Making the tabernacle. Exodus 25:1-9; 31:1-11; 39:32, 42, 43.

10. The great leader. You will want to speak very briefly of how Moses, listening constantly to the voice of God, was able to give his people the laws by which God wanted them to live. Tell how God led them safely through forty years of wandering in the wilderness, until the time came when they were ready to enter the Promised Land of Canaan. There they were to establish a kingdom of people who would worship God and try to live in his way.

A Way to Proceed

Form the study groups. Give each the topic and reference from which they may get the information (see above). Points 1, 3, 4, 6, 8, and 9 call for six groups. You could have fewer groups by giving each two references. Or you can have fewer groups and give more of the story yourself.

Allow about twenty minutes for study. You will need to move from group to group, or have helpers do so, to be sure the boys and girls are getting a story line from the reference. They should be able to tell the story in a few simple statements for the whole group.

Presentation

Have the story of Moses from points 1-10 or from points 1-3 only, given by yourself or by the group which has prepared each.

If you go through point 10, have the whole group turn to Deuteronomy 6:4-6 in their Bibles, or on page 11 in the pupil's book. Have the reference read. Discuss ways in which the commandment "The LORD . . . might," may be kept in mind today. This may lead to memorization of the passage. The boys and girls might like to give a tableau reading of this for their final program. Let them discuss how they can pose a picture of Moses giving this teaching to a group of people, and having them repeat for him the key part of the verse. Or they may want to make a frieze-type poster of the words all running along in one line, decorated in brilliant colors or with spatter printing of leaf and flower forms.

Story: (If you choose to tell the story instead of assigning the guided study, you may divide it into two parts, or choose the parts you wish to tell.)

THE PRINCE WHO WAS ADOPTED

"There are too many of those children of Israel!" cried out the Pharaoh. "See to it that every boy that is born is killed."

There was wailing in the camps of the Israelites. Many boy babies were killed. But some escaped. The Pharaoh tried even harder to have them destroyed.

In one home a beautiful boy child was born. His mother was determined that he should be safe. She watched him tenderly and hid him when the soldiers were about. His older sister Miriam and his older brother Aaron kept watch and warned her.

But the day came when the baby's cries were so lusty that his mother knew they would be heard from a distance. She prayed to God and God helped her to think of a plan.

She wove a basket of reeds and smeared the inside with pitch which when dried would keep the water out. Then she lined it with soft cloths and put the baby into the basket. She carried it down to the tall reeds at the edge of the river where the princess came each day to bathe. The soldiers would not come near that place.

"Keep watch, Miriam. See that

43

nothing harms the baby," directed his mother.

Miriam played by the water. She never got out of sight of the basket floating among the reeds, swaying like a cradle as the wind moved the stalks.

Presently along came the princess. She reached the river bank. Almost at once she saw the basket floating among the reeds. "Fetch it here! We'll see what's in it!" she directed.

One of her maids waded out into the water. She carried the basket to the princess. When its cover was lifted, there was a beautiful baby boy. He was howling with indignation and perhaps hunger.

"It's a Hebrew child," cried the princess. "Isn't he a darling? I'm going to keep him for my very own."

"Do you want a nurse for him, Princess?" asked Miriam who had crept up close. "Yes," said the princess. "I'll have to have a nurse." Her eyes twinkled. "Do you by any chance know of one who would take care of the baby for me?"

Miriam nodded. Then she ran and brought the baby's own mother. The princess laughed to see how eagerly the crying baby greeted someone who was supposed to be a stranger to him.

"Take him and raise him," she said. "I'm going to name him Moses because I took him out of the water. When he's old enough, he shall come to the palace and be a little prince. I'll adopt him."

So Moses lived at home till he was old enough. Then he went to the palace. There he was trained as any other little prince was trained. He was taught all the wisdom of the Egyptians but he never worshiped their gods. He worshiped God about whom his mother and his father taught him, and to whom they prayed.

* * *

Moses grew to be a man. He saw his own people, the Hebrews, being mistreated by the Egyptians. He saw them slaving to make bricks for the buildings the Egyptians were forever putting up. He saw the cruelty of the overseers. Moses could hardly stand it.

One day in a lonely spot he found an Egyptian overseer mistreating a Hebrew. Moses looked around. Not a person was in sight, so he killed the Egyptian. He buried his body in the sand. It was an ordinary enough thing for a prince to do in that land. Nobody would think much about it. "And besides," thought Moses, "nobody will know."

But he was mistaken. The rescued Hebrew must have talked, for the very next day when Moses tried to settle a quarrel between two Hebrews, one of them said, "Are you going to kill us, as you did the Egyptian?"

After all, Moses was not an Egyptian. He was a Hebrew, and killing an Egyptian was not exactly what would be smiled upon by the Pharaoh.

Moses left in a hurry. He traveled as far as he could and finally left Egypt behind. He went on and on, until he felt he would be safe. Now he was no longer a rich and pampered prince. He was just a weary, hungry traveler, with no place to stay.

One evening he sat down by a well. Shepherds came to water their sheep. First came the seven daughters of Jethro. But as soon as the men shepherds came they began to drive away the girls and their sheep. Moses couldn't stand that. He got up and ordered the men to stand aside until the girls had finished. Moses was used to being obeyed. He spoke like a prince, with authority. The men shepherds gave in. They stood sullenly by, while the girls watered their sheep.

When the girls got home much earlier than usual, their father asked how it happened, and they told him about the young man who had helped them. "Did you ask him to come home with you?" asked Jethro.

He sent them back to bring Moses.

Jethro was the priest of Midian and in his house Moses found welcome and refuge. He became the shepherd of Jethro's sheep, and he married one of the seven daughters.

* * * *

Moses was not to be a shepherd for the rest of his life.

The Pharaoh who had oppressed the Hebrews died. But things were no better under his successor and the people cried to God to remember them in their distress. Now God had a leader who could lead the Hebrews out of slavery. He had a man who could rule over them as they moved into the wilderness. He had a man of loyalty and faith and courage. But would that man undertake God's task? Would he be willing to risk his life and give all he had to doing God's work?

* * * *

Moses was tending his flock out in the wastelands where there was some pasture and water holes when he saw what he thought was a flaming bush. The bright flames leaped up, but the bush was not burned. Moses went to see what it was.

Then the voice of God spoke to him. God called to him to go to Egypt and rescue his people, and to lead them back into the Land of Promise that God had promised to Abraham and to his descendants forever.

Moses was unwilling. He made one excuse after another.

In the end, however, he bowed his head and accepted God's call. He gave his heart and his mind to doing the seemingly impossible thing that God was asking of him.

* * * *

It was no easy thing to accomplish the freedom of the Hebrew people. God sent plagues, storms, and sickness. Pharaoh would not grant freedom. God gave Moses power to perform wonders to prove that his God was a God of power and might.

At last the day came when the Pharaoh finally gave consent for the people to leave. The Egyptians loaded them with gold and silver. "Get out and be gone," they cried. "Take anything. Just be away! We can stand this no longer."

The Hebrews were ready to go. They had their possessions packed as Moses had directed them, and they streamed out toward the road to freedom. There were the men, thousands of them, and the women and children. There were flocks and herds. It was a great company. Directing them was Moses and his older brother, Aaron. The elders of the people led the tribes. They were on their way.

* * * *

Almost at once the Pharaoh regretted letting the slave-tribes go.

He gathered his army and went after them. He found them camped on the borders of the Red Sea. Then God caused a great wind to blow. The wind whipped back the waters of the shallow sea, until the Hebrews could see the bottom. "Come," cried Moses. He led them through the bed of the sea, with the wind blasting at them but keeping the waters from covering them. So they came to safety, and the wind died down. The waters rolled back and destroyed the faithless Pharaoh and his soldiers.

Leading the Hebrews to safety was the least of Moses' work. He must lead them to know God's laws, and to become a people faithful to him. It soon became apparent that the people were not yet ready to go into their Promised Land. They did not trust God. They kept making idols and images of gods of the people they had lived among and offering gifts and prayers before those images.

"They will have to wander in the wastelands for forty years," said God, "until they learn to trust and obey."

Thus the wilderness became their home, and they lived in tents, moving from one place to another and always looking for water for their flocks and pasture for their herds.

Moses spent hours and days alone with God up in the bare, desolate mountains. He spent long hours in prayer and in meditation.

God showed him what was the right way. He showed him how the people must live and what they must believe.

Moses told the people all that he learned from God.

One of the great teachings Moses gave the people was quoted by Jesus many hundreds of years later as the greatest of all the commandments:

"Hear, O Israel: The LORD our God is one LORD; and you shall love the LORD your God with all your heart, and with all your soul, and with all your might."—Deuteronomy 6:4-5.

He told them how they were to teach their children about God and cause them to love him and to obey him and to walk in his ways.

* * * *

The Egyptians had had wonderful temples in which to worship their gods. The Hebrews had no consecrated place, so God planned for them a marvelous tent of worship, that could be carried with them wherever they went.

Moses directed the building of the tent.

The great craftsman Bezalel trained workers to make marvels of gold and silver, of bronze and copper. He had them make woven materials, rich and fair to look upon, and strong to withstand the winds and sands of the desert. In the temple were golden and bronze and silver vessels and ornaments. The robes of the priests were rich and decorated with precious stones.

It was a wonderful day when the Hebrews dedicated their tabernacle, as the worship tent came to be called. They felt the glory of God within it, and they knew that God was still with them even though they had not reached the Promised Land.

* * * *

Through forty years of wanderings in the wilderness, Moses taught the people. He gave them laws to live by. He gave them the great Ten Commandments. Moses also gave them rules for every day. He told them how they were to live when they reached the Promised Land. He reminded them constantly of God's love and goodness to them. He reminded them that when they lived as God's people, keeping the laws of God and being righteous, the blessing of God was with them. But when they forgot God and wandered off into the evil ways of the people round about them, God's blessing could not be with them.

* * * *

Moses was aged and near the end of his work. God led him into a high mountain. From there God showed Moses all the land which he had promised to Abraham and to his children for ever.

Moses saw the land laid out before his eyes. As he looked out over Canaan, Moses knew his work was completed. On the mountain he died, but he left behind him a people ready to go into the land of promise and a new leader ready to guide them.

Never would the people forget Moses, their great prophet and teacher. Never would they forget how God had used him to lead his people from slavery in Egypt and how he had made them into a strong people, ready to go forward as God would have them go.

Playing Out Scenes from Moses' Story

If you told the juniors the story, either from the pupil's book, or from this text, you may want to substitute playing out the first part of the story for the research time.

If you had the story looked up by the boys and girls, you will have to omit the dramatization, or substitute it for some of the activities suggested for work time.

Four groups may work out these four scenes: The rescue of Moses by the princess (all girls); Moses trying to settle a quarrel (all boys); Moses and the daughters of Jethro, and the unpleasant men shepherds (boys and girls); Moses in the wilderness (1 boy). This last may be part of the "I am" presentations, with Moses thinking about what his life has been and how now God has called him to a great task and he is willing to go back into Egypt and even to risk his life to do God's will.

These scenes would work out equally well with puppets and the research necessary to plan costumes then would take the place of other research.

Recreation

The games committee may lead in a period of games or some other kind of recreation.

Having Fun with Work

Some unfinished work from last session may be completed by all or by some of the juniors.

"I am Moses," may be started, or the scenes from the early life of Moses may be worked into little playlets. Or the scene of Moses giving the great commandment to the people of Israel may be planned. This will depend on whether you told the story or did research and also on whether you used the Moses story as a whole or just the first part of it.

Learning the hymn on which work was started earlier may continue.

If working out Deuteronomy 6:4-6 as a scene appealed to the juniors, this may be the first scripture they learn by heart. This is a good phrase to use with juniors. They are not to memorize coldly, but with their hearts as well as their minds. You may suggest, instead of the scene of Moses teaching the people, or in addition to it, "Moses said the people were to write this commandment on their doorposts and on their gates. They did so, putting the writing in little boxes to keep it safe. We might make a lovely big scroll with these words, if you like, and decorate it with drawings and paintings of flowers and leaves. Or you might each make a copy to take home and put on the doorway of your bedroom." You might suggest that writing a commandment in one's heart, by learning it, is the best way of all of remembering God's word to us. Likely the juniors might be interested at this point in leafing through their books and finding other directions or laws that God has given us through the great leaders of Bible times. They may choose one of these to make a scroll, or frieze, or to memorize. Not all juniors need to learn the same verses, although all should be familiar with one if they want to use it in dramatization or worship.

Notice that there are several types of manual activity which may occupy the juniors today. They are clay modeling; time line (making pictures of Moses' story, or word accounts of it; see Activity Sheet No. 5 if you are using the sheets); frieze poster of Moses' words with spatter print or other decorations; puppets for any of the playlets or dramatizations; continuing with making a tent life set-up (this will be very usable for the wilderness-dwelling period); adding to the worship booklets. You will emphasize what best develops the thought of the session for your pupils and what gives them deepest enjoyment and satisfaction, and encourage them to choose such activities.

Save some time for each junior, or pair of juniors, to plan questions that might possibly "stump" the "other side" in a quiz tomorrow. Each junior should check with you, or with a helper to see whether the question he has devised is a fair one. You, or an assistant must be ready to write out the questions the younger ones have thought up. Don't waste their time in laborious writing —thinking up the question is their part of the job.

Putting things carefully in order is part of the work time. If it is not necessary to put materials away, you might say, "Suppose someone comes in. They can enjoy what we have been doing and learn a lot from it if we arrange it almost like a museum that is taking shape!" This may encourage the juniors to want to print explanatory cards to go with such things as their clay tablets.

Worship Suggestions

The juniors may gather quietly for worship now. Or, you may have decided to have worship following the story or the study of Moses, before any activities are followed through.

The adult who is to lead worship must be ready to take advantage of any development of thought during the session to this point, so as to lead from it into the worship experience for the juniors.

Probably the worship scripture, hymn, and prayer, used last session, should be used again today. Juniors may use their worship books if they are making them, or the charts or posters you have made for words of response and so forth.

The leader may wish to say something like this: "The Bible is God's record for us. In it he tells how he reached out in love to the people of the world and chose first one family and then many families to form a nation that would be devoted to his purposes. Through them he could bless all the families of the earth. But the Bible is not just a book of history. It is also God's word to us today.

"We have been thinking and learning about Moses. God had a task for him to do. God has a task for each of us to do. Sometimes it is a big task he has in mind, sometimes just a little one. If we listen to God's voice as it comes to us through the Bible and if we pay attention to his guidance in our hearts and minds, each one of us can be prepared by God, as he prepared Moses, to do the thing he wants us to do. In these days together, let us all have our minds and hearts open to hear God's word to us, and give him our love and loyalty as we try day by day to live in his way. Then we will grow more able to do what he wants of us, each day of our lives."

Conversation About the Session

The juniors should be ready now to evaluate the day's work. You may ask, "Has our session helped you see how God plans for and works with people? Why do you think God was concerned about those slaves in Egypt? What promise had he made to Abraham? Why was it important for the people or children of Israel, as they were called, to move back into the Promised Land? What would God do for the peoples of the earth if a nation grew up that was faithful to him and that wanted to live in his way? Do you think the world needed strong families who were faithful to God? Does the world today need them? What have we learned today that helps you to think so?" As the juniors answer these or similar questions you may guide them to feel more strongly that God, in his wonderful plan for mankind, was establishing a people through whom he could speak to the families of the earth, just as through Abraham he had spoken to the one family. They may see, too, that leader after leader would be needed to respond to God's call for someone to guide the people.

Reading Deuteronomy 6:4-6 might follow this conversation. It may be read in unison from the pupil's book, page 11.

The reading may be followed by singing, or reading if the tune is not known, "The God of Abraham Praise," page 7 of the pupil's book.

The leader may offer a prayer of thankfulness for God's wonderful guidance in the past, and especially for his guidance for us through the Lord Jesus Christ.

If another hymn is desired choose it from the list on page 124. You may wish to conclude with the offering service and the benediction.

Closing Time

Make any announcements needed. When restrictions have to be given, try to give at least one good reason for the restriction and ask for the happy co-operation of the entire group in observing it. If you have something planned for activities or games or in the way of study that will appeal especially to the juniors, be sure to stress it to encourage their return the next time.

POSSIBLE STEPS IN PLANNING

Read through this session's projected procedures and next session's as well. That will help you to decide what you are going to do with the Moses story.

The simplest thing is to tell, in the first session, the story up to the time when he was watching the sheep and saw the burning bush, and then do puppet or live dramatizations of the scenes of his early life. Then use the rest of the story in the next session.

Probably the second easiest is to tell the whole story of Moses, this time, and then next time recall the latter part of it. Relate activities today to the early life and next session to the latter part of his life.

Learning the story by research is hardest and is suitable only for older juniors. It can be done as a whole, or in two parts as described in the session plans.

Put down in your notebook the steps which will be followed in procedures according to the plan you choose.

Then read your scripture background, and prepare your story or your plan for research. (The scripture given for research will provide your own scripture background.)

Go carefully over the introduction to the story. Remember that we are not giving our juniors just a number of stories. We are guiding them to see how God used men who had the faith and loyalty to follow the way he pointed out, who had the courage or devotion to undertake the tasks he set them. The juniors will appreciate the stories more if they are guided to hear them in the light of the introduction you make.

Worship should be the high point of the session. The one who is to lead it should be most carefully prepared. You may find that you wish to work along lines other than those suggested, and you are free to do so. Work with the committee may this time consist of consulting them about how to handle use of the pupil's book in worship, about which hymn from page 124 will best fit into the thought of the service you have planned, about whether to read as a poem or sing "The God of Abraham Praise." Your committee may suggest beginning to learn this hymn as early-comers arrive so as to be able to use it with music in a later service, if not today. If juniors are to take the offering, they may want to practice doing it so that they can move smoothly.

Do not limit worship to this planned service. Whenever there is a moment that seems right for it, a prayer, a verse of praise, or a unison reading may be brought into the procedures. We cannot suggest where this will be, for it is a most intimate thing and only you who are working with your group will sense the right moment and what to do in it. One junior leader had many song-verses at her command and her sessions were rich with spontaneous music of praise in which all joined heartily. Another knew by heart so many scripture verses that she could voice the feeling of the group whenever doing so through scripture would enhance the session.

You will need to check on what the games committee is doing or will do on this second morning. Do not leave too much planning to them at first. The adult leader will need to have ideas in mind to guide them. He should be thoroughly familiar with all the suggestions given under Recreation on page 121 and be prepared to help the committee begin to look ahead and schedule the sort of recreation they want for the rest of the week. If there is no committee, the helper who will conduct games should work out a tentative schedule for the week and detailed plans for Session 2.

If you plan to send home the pupil's books at the close of this session or the next, be sure to sign your name to the letter to parents on the last page of the book.

Guided activities need planning at two points. There are those in which *all* children will want to take part, such as making their worship books or choosing what they want to do with the memory passage. For these your motivating introductions are all important. "We have just five minutes in which to paste these prayers onto page ____ of your worship books," puts the emphasis where it belongs onto a speedy doing of a small chore. The prayer already typed out and trimmed to size, paste, the worship books, and so forth are all ready. The juniors will simply fly to get it done.

Then there are activities in which some children are doing one thing, some another. Some may like clay work and want to make tablets with other Bible verses. See Activity Sheet No. 4 if you are using the sheets for directions. Some may like making scenes and posters with the figures from Activity Sheet No. 7. Some may like puppet or live dramatization. Some may like map work. Some may enjoy drawing for the time line or for a frieze. Some may like decorative work as for the frieze poster of the words of the Great Commandment. Let the pupils choose what they wish to do.

Your problem is to consider which of these you will list under "The children may, today—" in your notebook. If you plan to have all these things available for their choice, supplies must be in excellent order and helpers assigned to groups which need constant help, such as dramatization groups.

Your set-up for work this first day or two is important. It sets the pattern for easy, relaxed, effective work on the part of the children, your helpers, and yourself. If something went wrong yesterday, do not just lament it. Find out why it went wrong. At what point did things begin to move in the wrong direction? Was it something you need to work at, or was it something you can forget about but not let happen again?

The most vital part of your preparation is to think deeply about God's great purpose as it unfolds and about what he asked of each man you are to study and the way in which they responded to his loving trust in their loyalty and willingness. Remember that you are set to a task by him, which may seem difficult and heavy, but which will advance his mighty purposes as you go forward confidently, giving all you have to it in the days ahead.

Go Down, Moses!

The Whole Study shows how, under God, people can accomplish what would be impossible for them were it not for their trust in God and the help that he gives those willing to undertake his work.

We Follow Moses as he finally accepts God's plan for his life and becomes the great leader and lawgiver of God's people as they become a nation that will witness for him.

The Story of how Moses resisted when first confronted with God's purpose, but finally yielded and gave himself to its accomplishment is found in Exodus 3:2—40:38 and in the Book of Deuteronomy. It is also given in outline in Hebrews 11:23-28. You will refer specifically to Exodus 18:6, 12, 13-27; 32:1-6, 15-20; 25:1-9; 22:25—23:12; 20:1-17; Deuteronomy 6:4-9; Exodus 35:30—36:5; Deuteronomy 4:15-24; 7:6-9; 8:8-20. References are given here in the order of their use.

The Juniors, as they follow the story of Moses, should come to feel more clearly that God's laws are good and wise, and that those who are loyal to them are witnessing for God and showing their love and devotion for him.

HIGHLIGHTS FOR THE THIRD SESSION

Early arrivals:

Work on games, worship, special committees
Look at work begun and continuing with it
Prepare costumes for dramatizations

Class Activities:

Adding to worship books
Quiz time: With two sections, just for fun
Dramatizations from last session
Story: "Moses Faces the Pharaoh!"
Research: into Moses' work in the wilderness
Reports on research

Recreation (as planned by committee)

Having Fun with Work

1. Setting up the beginning of an exhibit
2. Practicing choral reading
3. Continuing "I am . . . ."
4. Beginning memory work
5. Adding to the quiz questions from today's study
6. Preparing time line for next session

Worship (using scripture and songs from the course)

Closing Time

PLANNING FOR THE THIRD DAY

You may be continuing the study using the response of Moses to God's challenge. How far along you are depends on what happened last session. You may have told the entire story and planned to *start* certain activities today. The possible session plan given now is designed to help you if you are telling the story and doing the work in two parts. Do not be bound by it. Twist it, turn, and change it. Use it but don't be hampered by it.

Specific suggestions for planning come after the session suggestions.

A POSSIBLE SESSION PLAN

As the Juniors Come

The games committee with their teacher leader will want to continue work on planning game time. The committee may want to try out some games to be sure they understand the rules clearly. They may want to arrange for equipment or make things, such as beanbags.

The worship committee also will meet with the adult leader to help prepare for worship. See suggestions under "Worship."

Other juniors may enjoy looking at what was started the previous session. They may want to browse among books and pictures. Someone may want to "just finish up" something that was almost completed yesterday. If dramatizations are to be given, some may plan costumes with an adviser while others practice with puppets. Some may learn hymns suggested by the worship committee.

Any materials to be used for worship today may be added to the worship books, or printed out on large sheets of paper or a chalkboard. Pictures of Moses' life may be found and posted.

Quiz Time

The questions the juniors devised earlier will be used for fun with a quiz, having two sides to compete. If you wish, questions from the first day may be included.

Dramatization from Last Session

Any dramatization worked on last session may be given if it is ready. If you need more time to get ready, you may omit this now, and plan for the presentation after the work time. In any case those preparing such dramatizations should announce their plans.

Story

The second half of the story of Moses, page 45 from Session 2, may now be told if it was not used last time. If it was used, recall it briefly. Then go on with the research in the Bible.

Research

You may say, "God had chosen Moses to free his people from slavery in Egypt. But long years of leadership were needed to help them become ready to go into the Promised Land and become a nation. Let's go to our Bibles and find answers to some questions."

The questions with the references may be written on slips of paper ahead of time and handed out now. Two to three boys and girls may work at each reference. If you have a large group give question and reference to two or even three small groups and let each be ready to add to what the others report if something is left out.

1. Who was to settle quarrels and decide which one was right if two men were quarreling? Exodus 18:6, 12, 13-27. Do you think Jethro's was a good plan?

2. Did the people always remain faithful to God? Exodus 32:1-6, 15-20.

3. What did God lead Moses to teach the people about making offerings? Exodus 25:1-9. Why did they need a sanctuary like that?

4. Did Moses have to make practical laws for the people? Exodus 22:25—23:12.

5. How many of the Ten Commandments that God gave Moses to give to the people can you remember? Exodus 20:1-17.

6. Did Moses give the people any responsibility for teaching God's laws to their children? What would be the most important law? Deuteronomy 6:4-9.

7. Did Moses have helpers? Exodus 35:30—36:5.

8. The people all around worshiped many gods. What did Moses teach about making images to worship? Deuteronomy 4:15-24.

9. What did Moses teach the people about God's love for them? Deuteronomy 7:6-9; 8:8-20.

Reports on Research

Each group may take three minutes to tell what they found out. (You may have had research only on two or three questions if desired.) Each will read its question and give its answer.

You may conclude: "God had called Moses to do an almost impossible task—first to free the people from slavery, and then to guide them to become a devoted people who listened to God's laws. But they were not always faithful and they suffered wars and exile. In the end, however, centuries after Moses' day, the Hebrews became a people who refused ever to worship anyone but God. Of all the people on the earth they had the highest understanding of God and his ways. Finally, God sent Jesus to reveal the way of righteousness and love.

Recreation

Under the direction of the games committee.

Fun with Work

You may be continuing any of the activities started earlier. Sometimes a committee may be chosen to finish a job while others begin new activities. Likely, dramatizations can be continued by those who have parts in them while the rest of the group do other things.

On this day the entire group may plan out its work time. "We need three people to work on costumes for the puppets." Or "We want to try a choral reading of one of the psalms. Would you like to begin or end our work period with that?" Or "There are several passages we can begin to memorize. Would you like a committee to choose one for us to work on later today?" And, "Who would like to represent Moses as a leader in our 'I am' series?" Perhaps you need to state, "Our nomad village or shepherd scene needs more figures. Who would like to finish that?" Or, "I'd like two boys to bring the time line up to date."

A helper may write on the chalkboard the names of the boys and girls who want to undertake certain things, and then each can get busily to work. Be sure to be ready with something else for those who finish an undertaking. Someone might like to draw extra pictures for the time line; or work out a new small scene with puppets; or decorate a scripture passage done in manuscript writing.

Either before or after these individual and small group undertakings two things are to be done by the entire group.

First is the choral reading, from the juniors' books, page 16. You may say, "Until just recently, in most of our churches, only two ways of reading Bible passages were used. One person read the passage, or the minister and the people read verse and verse about. Of course sometimes a whole group recited together as if it were one voice. Lately, however, people have been trying a new way of bringing out the beauty and meaning of some scripture passages. This is called choral reading. It is like an anthem except that there is no music. Would you like to try a very simple choral reading that is found in your books?"

Have the juniors turn to page 16 of their books. Help them divide into two groups, light (or high) voices and dark (or low) voices. Then begin reading. Guide them to see how the thought expressed by one group leads to the next, or how the second group answers the first. If your group has done choral reading before, they may wish to elaborate on the arrangement. One voice, two voices, three voices, may take over some of the parts now assigned to light voices. All voices may come in following one, two, or three voices. Encourage the juniors to feel the worship that is in these lovely expressions of devotion to God. Without doubt someone will suggest using this in worship, and perfecting it will be stimulated by the desire to use it in this way. The juniors may work for smoothness of utterance. Variation can also be secured by saying some things softly and others in full voice. Those of you who are familiar with choral reading often do not need directions. The juniors may wish to memorize the passage and, if so, you may want to suggest that they do so later in the year since full memorization by each pupil now could be disastrous to the choral reading unless books are used for the latter.

Second is the choice by individuals, or by the group, of some other biblical passage they would like to learn. Pupils may find something in their books. They may decide that they would like to learn the lovely passage, Amos 5:8, on page 2 of their books. This could be used as a response in worship, or as something to think of first thing in the morning or late at night when they go to bed. Or the passage from 1 Peter 3:10-12 may be chosen because it helps to know God's way in daily life. You may introduce the idea of choosing and learning by heart with some such statement as: "All through the years people have found in the Bible God's word to them. They have not been content to read it just once in a while. They have wanted to learn scripture by heart so that it would come into their minds when it was needed. You may like to choose a passage from the Bible by looking at one or two printed in your book. You may like to learn it so that it is in your heart as well as in your mind. Look at pages 2 and 6 and 11 and 15 and read the Bible passages there. Think of times when you could use them if you just knew them." The juniors will choose and may decide whether to learn as a group or to have individual learning.

Preparing a Quiz

A quick distribution of pencils and slips of paper will enable each of the juniors to contribute a question for a quiz for next session. Remind them to make the questions clear and such that the answers can be short. You will gather the slips of paper and a helper can make up the quiz using these questions and others if you feel they are needed.

Summary and Discussion

You may want to give a brief summary. Recall that God was able to move forward in his great purpose of having first a family and then a people as witnesses for him in the world. The leader Moses was a witness because he was willing to devote himself to carrying out God's purposes, and was ready at all times to receive God's guidance. Point out that Moses had been given, by God's design, the training that would make him able to lead a great people. Help the group recall that he gave all his abilities and all his life to working the laws that God gave him into the lives of the people, and training them to become truly loyal to God. You may wish to ask the juniors to tell what has meant most to them of the things you have done this day. Comment on their increased ability as they, too, have tried to live as children of God and to follow in his ways.

Worship

Use the same opening scripture used previously or one of those suggested on page 124 (see "Worshiping Together," page 123). One of the thoughts for worship given on page 124 may be used, linking the thought of God's wisdom in giving his people his laws through Moses, with his wonderful plan for the world about us. A hymn from page 124 or some other appropriate hymn may be used. If "The God of Abraham Praise" is learned or is known, it would fit in well. The verses from Amos at the beginning of the pupil's book would work excellently into such a program. The choral reading (page 16, pupil's book) worked on earlier today may be ready to use in worship. Juniors may participate as indicated in the suggestions under "Worshiping Together," and elsewhere.

Closing Time

If there is to be something special to end the first five days, or some event to which all will look forward, announce it now. Make any comments on the way plans have worked out. Express appreciation for co-operation. If behavior reminders have to be made, let them be gay and "comfortable" as well as specific and firm.

POSSIBLE STEPS IN PLANNING

As you begin to get ready for this third day, take stock first. How are you getting along with helping the juniors feel that God has a great purpose for the world and that he uses men and women of courage, devotion, faith, and loyalty to carry forward that purpose? Are you and your helpers, as you work with the boys and girls, able to guide their thinking so that they admire, appreciate, want to do likewise? Do you see evidence that they wish to act in such ways as will increase their ability to be good leaders or good followers in the work of God today? It is easy to do the mechanical things, but harder, though rewarding, to guide a child toward a response to God.

Evaluate what you have done in the way of the various procedures. Is the quiz fun? Would it be more fun if you worked out the questions rather than have the juniors do it? Would a small committee like to be a quiz panel to think up both hard and easy questions for a quiz next session? Who would be the best one to help them? When would they work?

How is the story going? Are you telling it well? Does it grip the attention of the juniors? Are you making Moses stand out as a grand person?

How is worship working out? Is it a time of reverent feeling that God is near? Are you using children without enough preparation? Are there parts of the worship that could be more worshipful with better training of juniors who are to take part? Are you helping the boys and girls feel at home in public prayer? Is every helper worshiping right with the children?

How is the game-planning progressing? Does equipment need to be made or borrowed for tomorrow? Who will be responsible? Are there any problems? Is everyone playing fair? Are there any "bullies"? How are you to meet and solve any such problems? Do you have handicapped children? Are special games being planned for them? Or do they enjoy watching the others more than participating fully in games of their own?

At what stage is each activity? Will the shepherd scene be in the final exhibit? By the way, have you even suggested to the juniors that they may have a final exhibit? Would it be well to list periodically the things the juniors decide should be in the exhibit on the last day?

Are you picking up ideas from the first session and using them? For instance, a clay-tablet invitation to another group to join in worship or games would let the juniors see how the clay tablets were put to very practical use, and would be a novel way of inviting the others. Have you found other uses for the clay, such as making jars, or other props for your table-top scenes?

Have you an adequate supply of pictures for background for the Bible stories? If not, would the juniors like to build pictures by painting backgrounds and then pasting some of the figures from

Activity Sheet No. 7 on the background to illustrate the scene they want to portray? Sometimes juniors like to illustrate a story with their own drawings.

Is the map work to go on? A Bible atlas will show where to draw the lines roughly to indicate the escape from Egypt and the wanderings in the wilderness. Let the juniors look up this information. It is their job to find and transfer it; yours, to show them where to find it.

Are your basic supplies in good shape? Do you need to put some things in another place to prevent a crowd pushing all at once to get crayons and paper, or anything else?

Have you taken the quiz questions the children made, and worked them up into a quiz for this session?

Are special supplies for whatever activity you have chosen at hand? Have you some emergency supplies for occupying the rebel who will not work with the rest?

How is your notebook? Does it have the jottings that will help you to carry out your own plans for a fruitful session next time?

Just a lot of questions? Yes, but when you have answered each in turn, and have asked yourself others that rise because of your particular situation, you will find yourself ready.

Above all, was it fun? Did your eyes sparkle with satisfaction as you saw the children fairly grow in Christian understanding, wisdom, ability, and new attitudes before your eyes? Your plans for tomorrow should hold even more promise toward that end.

He Shall Sing of Me to My People

The Whole Study is about people who have been called to serve God in many different ways according to their abilities.

We Begin the study of David, the shepherd lad, who even as a lad was so atune to God that God knew he would be able to call him to a great task; and we find out how, even in the time of preparation, he asked for God's guidance and acted as "a man after God's own heart."

The Story of David in his early years is found in 1 Samuel 16:1—31:8. Specifically you may use: 16:1-13, 14-23; 18:1-9, 12-16; 10:8-10, 18; 20:1-11, 24-42; 22:1-2; 23:1-5; ch. 24; 31:1-2, 8.

The Juniors through this day's study should come to feel that they, too, can listen to God's word as they grow toward greater understanding and knowledge of God; and that they need to act, right now, in accordance with the will of God, preparing themselves for whatever he would have them do.

HIGHLIGHTS FOR THE FOURTH SESSION

Early arrivals:

Work on games, exhibit, and worship committees

Look at pictures and story books about David

Class Activities

Quiz time

Work on Choral Reading

Story: "David and King Saul"

Research: Shepherd life in Judah

More incidents of David's life (from the Bible)

Reports on Research

Recreation

Having Fun with Work

1. Continuing with the exhibit: shepherd life
2. Choral reading
3. Practicing memory work

4. Adding to the quiz questions
5. Continuing "I am . . ."
6. Planning a dramatization about David
7. Something special for tomorrow

Worship (as planned by the committee)

Closing time

PLANNING FOR THE FOURTH DAY

The fourth and fifth days may be spent studying about David. The juniors will love to hear about his adventurous life. David's story breaks into a number of small stories. Perhaps you will want to take them one by one, and follow each with activities connected with it. Perhaps you will want to tell the whole story at the beginning and then spend the rest of the day and the fifth day following up, talking over, doing things connected with parts of the story. The steps in planning and the procedures are based on telling part of the story the fourth day and the rest on the fifth day. You will have to make your own decision as to which of the three plans is best for your group. Read the suggested procedures *for both days* before you decide. Then use "Steps in Planning," found after the session plans and make your own plan in your notebook.

A POSSIBLE SESSION PLAN

As the Juniors Come

If you have found the juniors like committees, the games committee and others may get to work as soon as even one or two members are present. The games committee should work out something that will be specially good fun for the last session for the week. They can complete details tomorrow morning, but the planning should be done today.

Other juniors may choose to help you set things up, to find pictures of David's life, to browse among books and atlases, to add to their worship books and those of the people in committee work, or to sing around the piano. This is an excellent time for you to have informal conversation with individual children or two or three as they work, finding out what their interests are, about their problems, and guiding them to want to do the things that will help them grow in Christian ways.

Quiz Time

Spend a few minutes on the quiz you prepared from the questions the juniors wrote in the last session, or, if a quiz panel was set up, let the juniors conduct the quiz.

Choral Reading

Experiment with different ways of using the Psalm of Praise on page 16 of the pupil's book. See suggestions for choral reading on page 58. Let the juniors make suggestions about how to get different effects. They may plan to use the reading in worship next week, or to have it listed as a possible item for a program for their parents.

Story

See the story of David in the pupil's book. Use as much of the story as your plan requires. It may include the cave incident if you are breaking the story into two parts for this session and the next.

Thinking About David

You could ask the juniors to find out more about shepherd life in Old Testament days. Mention the reference books on Old Testament life and have the pupils hunt up more incidents in David's life from the Bible. But it will perhaps be more to the point to do a little thinking with them. You might ask, "What was there about David that helped God know he would make a good king for Israel?"

The juniors may think of various things, such as: David's modesty; the way he thought of God when he was alone with the sheep; his willingness to help Saul; his ability to make people his friends; his determination not to harm in any way the one whom God had made king of Israel; his courage; his leadership ability.

They may look at any pictures of David you have and get a feeling about this man who did not depend on his own strength, but was ready to be guided by God.

This would be a good time to find out whether the juniors would like to pose some picture scenes in the life of David. It would be a change from acting out a story. David can be posed as shepherd; as coming before King Saul; as playing on his harp;

65

as being given a rich cloak by Jonathan; as leading his men into hiding; as cutting off the piece from Saul's robe; as calling to Saul about it. Someone could read the parts of the story the scenes illustrate. Do not actually work out the scenes now. Just find out whether it is something the juniors would like to do and include it in your work time if they are interested. Scenes could be done with puppets, or pictures could be built up or drawn to illustrate the narrative, if the pupils prefer.

Reading a Psalm

Have the juniors turn to page 15 in their books. You may say, "David was a poet. He wrote psalms of praise to God. They probably were like many of the songs in our Book of Psalms. Part of Psalm 90 is given here. The poet was thinking of all those generations of men from Abraham on, who had trusted in God and found in him their help and refuge. Let us read the selection together." Do so. You may have a brief conversation about the thoughts in the psalm, guiding the juniors to feel that the words express our feeling too. God is still our "dwelling place," because without him we are in a world without sense or meaning. With him we are "at home" in the world he has made for us.

Recreation

As planned by the games committee. See p. 122.

Having Fun with Work

List on the chalkboard the different projects that are being worked on. The shepherd scene should be completed. A nomad camp might be added to the exhibit today. A Palestinian house with its flat roof is another possibility. A cave in a hill, with people "camping" in the mouth might be made.

If the map is being enlarged, the sites of Jerusalem and Bethlehem may be marked.

Are some still working with clay? It would be fine for making bricks or rocks to build a sheepfold and for the walls and parapet of the house. The flat roof may be made from heavy cardboard.

The scenes from David's life can be planned. Let the juniors choose and work them out. A committee may work up the running narrative to be read as the scenes are posed. Costume arrangement will take some time. As each scene is completed, all the juniors may stop what they are doing and look at it. There is no need to perfect any "scene" for presentation in a formal way.

One person may elect to create a David for the "I am . . ." series. He might choose to include a psalm for David to give as he tells about some one incident of his life. This might be included as one of the posed scenes with David himself speaking instead of the narrator.

If possible announce some special activity for the next session. It may be a hike with refreshments to take the place of the game-time. Or it may be having guests for worship or for games. It might be visiting one of the other departments. The juniors will need to plan how they will act and suggest how to make it a really good time for everyone.

If the pupils are still enjoying the quiz and like to make out the questions to "stump" each other, pass out pencils and papers for them to write their questions. Two or three may work together to make out questions if they wish.

Evaluation

Take a few minutes now for evaluation. You might ask, "Do you think we are succeeding in what we started out to do in these days together? Are we finding out more about God's purpose for people? (Let the juniors tell why they think they know more.) What other goals have we accomplished? (The boys and girls should be able to state that they have learned more about some of the great leaders of Bible times; about how God planned to work through them; about how they were willing to do as God wished and depended on his guidance and were loyal to him. They may want to mention having found out more about Bible times and about the people of those days. They should be helped to express their feeling of having a greater sense of God's purpose for the lives of each of us and of our need to try to know what God wishes us to do, and then to do it.) You may want to say, "God opens many, many doors of service. He gives us many opportunities at home, among our friends, in school, at church or church school, in fact wherever we are and whatever we are doing, to respond to his will for our lives. Each of us can and must decide many, many times whether we will go in God's way or in some easier way."

Worship

If the adult leader wishes, the conversation suggested under Evaluation may be worked instead into a conversation during worship. The junior worship committee may consider the questions and work out short answers to them to present at that time.

The choral reading may be used in worship today, even if it is not perfectly rendered. Hymns and prayer should be chosen to fit into the theme, "We Learn More of God's Way," if the suggestion of using the thoughts under "Evaluation" are used. If instead one of the ideas on page 125 is used, choose hymns and have prayers to fit the thought chosen. Psalm 90:1-4 may also be woven into the fabric of worship today.

Closing Time

You may want to make a statement today, something like this: "We've been thinking about how God planned to use people who could go ahead with courage and devotion to carry out his purposes on earth. It is comforting to realize that God isn't looking for someone who already had done something startlingly brave. Not at all. He looked around and found David, a boy who was doing the job his father asked him to do and was doing it well. On the side he had learned to play the harp. His thoughts always ran over with praise and love for God. God can use each of us. In these days we are all learning together how to be more aware that God is with us. We are learning skills. We are finding out in what ways people can help God carry out his purpose. Let us all remember as we go home that perhaps it is the hours when we are not here together that count most. What kind of persons are we trying to be all through each day? It's a happy thing to think that we can be workers for God just by the way we think and talk and act about the ordinary things of every day."

Any announcements that need to be made should be clearly stated.

Send them off with a "We're going to have a wonderful day tomorrow!" or some happy anticipation of the sort.

POSSIBLE STEPS IN PLANNING

First read the Bible background. Get to know David. Become clear about God's purpose for his life. Read his story as given in the pupil's book, page 12.

Now read the procedures in today's session and for tomorrow. Decide whether you will tell the whole story of David at first, or tell it in small sections followed by activities related to that part, or divide the story in two as the Possible Session Plans suggests. Jot down in your notebook a plan of your own, worked out from the ideas given or from previous experience you have had.

Consider the first three days of the school. What have the children enjoyed most and benefited from most? Plan to continue work along those lines. What activities will benefit from further work? Is it more important to complete them, or to start something new? (Dramatizations are often valuable just for the process of doing them, and completion to present them is not necessary.)

List in your notebook any problems that have risen, as, "Johnny is still unco-operative in committee work. Miss Stevens gets no response when she is guiding conversation. The noises from the playground make worship difficult." With your helpers study each problem. *Why* is Johnny unco-operative? How can you try to overcome his attitude? Are you being unreasonable and trying to force him into a groove? Or does he need firm handling for his own happiness? What shall we try tomorrow to get him to fit in better? Give Miss Stevens the help she needs, or, if necessary, let someone else try that part of the procedure. Make a note to change worship to a different hour, or work out some way to shut off the noise. Sometimes everyone has to agree to play quieter games.

Recall, for your own satisfaction, everything that went well. Rejoice together over every sign of growth on the part of the group or of individual children. This is just as important as solving problems. You need to delight in the good that is happening.

Now take a look at your program as you have planned it. Examine each task. Get ready for it. The story might be told by several persons today, each taking one part. Help the juniors see the long struggle as the people, who were only a dream when Abraham obeyed God's call, were led from loose tribal organization into a firm nation. Guide the pupils to feel their own responsibility for answering God's will for their own lives each day.

Recall each activity. Get clearly in mind the successive steps in working with each. Are any new materials needed?

Sometimes a different arrangement of working conditions helps. You may estimate how far along in the activity the juniors may go today and what will be a satisfying point at which to stop. Whenever possible let the boys and girls make the decisions about such things as the best way to continue, what is to be done next, and how the results of the work will be used. For instance, the worship committee may announce that they are planning to use the choral reading in worship, and ask everyone to help perfect it in the working part of the session. It may also be helpful for you to have an idea about how many juniors will be needed to "finish up" or "continue work today" on specific projects. You may then ask for volunteers—two for the map, six or eight for making pictures for the time line. If you are going to suggest a new activity, be sure you have directions for it clearly in mind, and all materials at hand that you need. If you plan a hike or picnic for next session be sure all is in order for it.

Your notebook should show just who is taking responsibility for each part of the day's leadership.

Your Power Shall Lead My People

The Whole Study shows how God works through individuals, who are willing to devote themselves to him, to lead people into a greater loyalty to him and to his purposes.

We Continue the story of David, seeing how he grew in his devotion to God, and how under God's guidance he made of his people a strong nation. We see him after he has sinned, earnestly seeking God's forgiveness in deep repentance. We find him to be one who leads his nation in worship of God and composes many psalms of praise for the worship of God.

The Story of David as king is found in the Book of 2 Samuel. Specific references you may want to use are: 2 Samuel 1:1-12; 2:1-7; 5:1-5, 9-12, 17-25; 6:12-15, 17-19; 7:1-17, 18-29; 8:15; 9:1-7; 11:14-15, 17, 26; 12:1-10, 13; 22:1-4, 17-26; 23:1-4; 24:18-25.

The Juniors, in addition to coming to know David better, should by this day's study be helped to want to lend themselves more fully to the guidance of God in their lives.

HIGHLIGHTS FOR THE FIFTH SESSION

Early Arrivals: Work on games, exhibit, worship, and special event committees. Finish up various activities.

Class Activities:

Quiz Time
Dramatization of Scenes in David's Life
Story: "David, the King"
Discussion (of David as a king true to his God)

Recreation (Perhaps a picnic or hike planned last session)

Having Fun with Work

1. Selecting and learning scripture passages
2. Adding to exhibits

3. Further work on dramatization
4. Continuing "I am . . ."
5. Putting away for the week end
6. Plans for sharing with others on Sunday
7. Instead of items 1-4, getting ready for and having the "Special Event" may fill this time

Worship: "God's Love and Power in Our Lives"

Closing Time

PLANNING FOR THE FIFTH DAY

Some of your planning was done as you got ready for the fourth day and decided just how to divide or arrange the study related to David. Your plans today will carry out and complete what started last session, or will take up the second part of the story. You may want to spend more time with David. Some activities may reach over into next week. Let this fifth session be meaningful, delightful, and absorbing for the juniors. On it will depend whether or not they come back next week. Detailed suggestions for planning are given after the possible session plans.

A POSSIBLE SESSION PLAN

As the Juniors Come

Your various committees may get right to work as soon as any of their members are present. You likely have worship, games, exhibit committees, and perhaps a committee for any special event that is to take place today. This will be a good time for having individuals or small groups finish up activities that need just a little more work. As usual, singing and looking at books and pictures and examining work done last session will be enjoyed by some of the boys and girls. Those presenting the dramatization will get ready.

Quiz Time

Use the questions prepared by the children or the teachers.

Dramatization

Those who worked on a dramatization or on posed scenes from the story of David may present them at this time. Perhaps this is one of the activities to list as a possible presentation for the final program. Make no hard-and-fast decision. A later dramatization may be the one actually chosen.

Conversation About Our Purposes

Establish the purpose for the session through conversation in which you recall with the juniors that our study is about God's choice of persons who would become able to help carry out his great purposes as they responded to his will for their lives. State that we continue to find out how David, whose story was begun yesterday, did so. Encourage the juniors to express their need to find out what God's purpose for their lives is, as God himself opens up in their hourly and daily life opportunities for choosing to live in his way.

Story

The part of David's story which deals with his work as king may be told now. You may want to introduce it in some way such as this: "God had chosen David the shepherd boy to be the next King of Israel. Saul had failed to do as God wanted. Would David do so? Would he be able to lead the people closer to God? Would he be open to God's guidance after he became a rich and powerful king? Or would he begin to depend on himself?"

Use the story as given in the pupil's book.

Conversation

After the story, let the juniors think about David's years of leadership as king and decide whether or not they themselves feel that he showed the courage to follow God's leadership, and the humility to acknowledge God as his leader. Did he ask forgiveness when he did what was wrong? Did he accept God's decisions for his life? They may decide whether he merited the name by which he is called by many people—"the Friend of God."

Recreation

As planned by the games committee (see p. 122).

Having Fun with Work

Begin today with group participation in memory work. If the passage first chosen is fairly well known, a second one, decided

73

on by the juniors, may be begun. Or, looking forward to the study of Amos which comes next, you might suggest that pupils illustrate Amos 5:8, which is printed at the beginning of the pupil's book. The juniors might divide into groups of six. Each group might make a series of illustrations, with each child taking one line. Stars, sunrise, a night scene, the sea, rain, and the words "The LORD is his name" decorated with a border or made in lovely decorated letters are the possibilities. Allow fifteen minutes for this, then let each group put up its pictures for the rest to look at. Each junior may repeat the part of the verse he has illustrated. Then all the juniors may move from one picture to another saying in unison the words that fit it. The verse will be learned before you know it.

Take time now for those who have prepared "I am Abraham," and "I am Moses," and "I am David" to give their presentations. If this is being done with puppets, ask for suggestions. Do the juniors want to prepare the same thing for men to be studied next week, or would they like to have an interview type of presentation, where one puppet represents a child of today? He would ask questions. Then another puppet representing Amos or Jeremiah or Peter or Paul would answer the questions. Juniors will probably be interested in the latter, and can look forward to it.

Any activities that are continuing may be worked on. If a new activity is desired, a diorama of David in the cave may be worked out. Or a rebus picture story of the life of David may be made. To do so, let the juniors make little pictures of every word in the story that can be pictured. *David* may be represented by a lad, at first, then a young man, then a crowned king. Words like sheep, spear, harp, king, enemy (massed spears), city, throne, friend (clasped hands) will be drawn instead of being written into the account. The juniors may write their own story, making it very simple, and including as many picture words as possible. If this is done on a large sheet of paper, pieces 2" x 2" may be used for drawing the pictures. They then can be pasted in place as pupils tell the story and you write it in big letters on the large sheet.

If some special event has been planned, you may want to omit "Fun with Work" and have whatever was planned for today.

Some pupils in vacation church schools plan to share with the children of the regular Sunday session some of the things they have been doing. If this has been cleared with the Sunday church school junior superintendent, some time may be taken during this work period to choose what to display, what to talk about, or what story or short talk or dramatization to give. If the children are from many different churches, there may be a difference in the sort of contribution which will be welcome, and choices must be made in accordance with that.

In many groups putting away for the week end is a little chore of which many hands make light work. If it is to be done by the juniors now, allow time for it.

Worship Suggestions

The theme for worship on this fifth day may be, "God's Love and Power in Our Lives." It should be the high point in the session. You might like to open with the responsive reading of Psalm 103:1, 2, 4, 22 as given on page 124 of this text. Follow this with a hymn of praise from the pupil's book. The Litany of Praise from page 21 of the pupil's book may be recited. The adult leader may want to make a short comment along these lines: "All this week we have been thinking about God's purpose for the lives of his children. We have seen how he was able to use the loyalty, faith, courage, and devotion of men whom he called to do for him the great tasks he had in mind. We have seen, too, how God has a purpose for each one of us, and how, like David the shepherd boy, we can make ourselves helpers for him just in doing the ordinary things of life in God's way. Through his wisdom and power God can make our lives strong and helpful if we open our hearts to his guidance and determine to do from hour to hour what God wants us to do." Choose from page 125 of this text a hymn that will help the juniors express their own desire to live daily under God's guidance and with his Spirit in their lives.

Closing

Be sure to express appreciation for the way in which the juniors have co-operated, recall the good time you have had together, announce some specially attractive feature for next week, and send the children home happy. In some groups some of the work done to date (unless it is to be used for the exhibit or in the last-day program or in usual procedures next week) is sent home today to encourage parents to sense some of the things that have been happening.

POSSIBLE STEPS IN PLANNING

What happens today depends on how you decided to handle the session on David's response to God's plan. Refer to your notebook for what you had jotted down. If you are following the sessions as outlined in this text, refer back to session four and note what you accomplished. Then look at the possible session plan to see what is suggested to follow it today. Read with especial care the paragraphs on purposes for both lessons. What further purposes can be attained beyond having the juniors learn more about David's career? Read the story of David again as given in the Bible, as well as the one in the pupil's book on page 12.

Study the list of activities and decide whether you need to start something new or give more time to something started earlier. Groups of juniors vary greatly. Some move slowly and need much more time to complete an undertaking to their satisfaction. Others move rapidly and enjoy a rather more sketchy but still satisfying experience of doing many things. Chart your own way.

As usual, the introduction to the story, the story itself, the conversation which follows and any dramatizations which reflect these activities should be planned carefully. Worship, by now, should be moving with reverence, without interruptions. Planned recreation should be contributing to the growth of the boys and girls. For some groups just a chance at playing is the ideal. For others conquering bad habits of temper, unfairness, selfishness, and other faults can take place through games. For still others, learning what fun many kinds of recreation can be is important. At this point, talk over with your helpers what your chief aim is, so the one to work with the games committee can guide its planning more effectively.

If the children plan to take some part of what they have been enjoying to their Sunday church school, clear with the superintendent in advance. You must ask if visitors will be welcome, exactly how much time they will be given, and what sort of presentation will be welcome. Puppet plays are usually popular. A junior can tell what is being studied, and announce that a certain scene from life will be shown by puppets. A choral reading may be done, a story told or dramatized, a poster shown and explained, or a song sung. Be very sure that one of the helpers is present to take care ahead of time of any staging needed for any presentation. If the children scatter to many churches and helpers cannot be with them, let them undertake only what will most likely be a happy experience.

Your work time must be carefully thought out. Some activities may run into next week. Sometimes it is helpful to plan it that way, as an invitation to come the second week. Items that have been made should be completed so they can be sent home, unless needed, as previously mentioned.

For children who enjoy drawing, the procedure suggested with the verse from Amos will be a change, since there will be as many times six ideas and drawings as you have groups of six children. Some junior groups have found color slides to be projected as they made comments; others have found pictures in the picture files. Use one of these ideas and, if you choose the second or third, be sure that among the pictures or slides the children examine there *are* those that will illustrate the lines.

Younger juniors may especially enjoy making the rebus story about David. A helper will print out the story, and the juniors will make the pictures to take the place of the words which can be replaced with drawings. Be sure to try this out in advance, but the ideas and the drawings should be the children's own.

If some special event has been planned to take up the usual work time, let all the details be planned, so that there is no confusion. Check on these now, so that you are sure of everything that is needed to carry out the plan.

If this is the day before a week-end break, do not wait for inspiration for your dismissal remarks. Know exactly what you want to say to send the children home happy and to encourage them to be back on Monday morning. If this is a once-a-week school, it is even more important, as the days go by, to say the right things at going-home time.

Go to Bethel!

This Entire Study deals with God's purpose for mankind, and his call to leaders of consecration and devotion to help bring his purpose and will before the people; it deals with the response of certain leaders to God's call, as they yielded their lives to his guidance and were shown how to do what seemed impossible tasks.

We Continue our study with the story of Amos, a simple shepherd God called to denounce the great powers of Israel and to prophesy the disaster that would befall them if they failed to heed God's law and live in God's way.

The Story of how God called Amos from being a herdsman, and of how he went to Bethel and spoke out for God is found in the Book of Amos. Specific references you may use are: Amos 1:1-5, 6, 9, 11, 13; 2:1, 4-8; 3:1-15; 5:8, 9, 16-17, 21-24; 7:10-15; 8:4-7.

The Juniors, as they learn of Amos and of his willingness to witness for God, may be encouraged to stand up for the right and to choose for themselves to do what is right.

HIGHLIGHTS FOR THE SIXTH SESSION

Early Arrivals:

Get ready for the session by getting out materials, choosing pictures, arranging room. Games committee may practice leading games. Worship committee may practice use of materials. Review the last five sessions' work.

Class Study:

Quiz Time (with panel of leaders)
Introduction to Story
Story: "Only a Herdsman"
Dramatic Reading (the story of Amos)
Evaluation and Planning Time

Recreation (You may take a five-minute rest period, then have a filmstrip on Amos)

Recall: "God's Purpose and Man's Response"

Having Fun with Work

1. Working on the exhibit: Diorama, or poster picture or frieze of Amos' story
   Continuing "I am . . ." preparation
2. Practicing memory work: What Amos said
3. Making time line additions
4. Planning quiz questions for next session

Worship: "Seek Good and not Evil"

Closing Time

PLANNING FOR THE SIXTH DAY

This sixth day may be a Monday following the week end, or it may be the sixth day of a once-a-week school; or some other plan may be in effect. You may wish to spread the study of Amos over two days and omit Jeremiah. If so, there is plenty to occupy the juniors for two days. But you will need to adapt the plans given under "Steps in Planning," found after the session plans. Read the Amos session and the Jeremiah session before deciding. The Jeremiah story could be used in worship in this session if you are going to omit the study of Jeremiah. For detailed suggestions see "Steps in Planning."

A POSSIBLE SIXTH-DAY SESSION

As the Juniors Come

You are delighted to see the juniors. Let them see your pleasure and feel your warmth in greeting them. You may have to get supplies and last week's work out of storage. Let them help you. Let them put up the big map, the litany, pictures; let them set up the things for the exhibit, and enjoy looking at what everyone did; let them get out the worship books, and begin to add to them if other items are to go in.

The games committee will be busy practicing for today although games may have been chosen.

The worship committee may meet with the adult leader for worship and go over any parts for which each is to have responsibility. They may want to help choose hymns that fit into the theme, or examine the scripture passages in the pupil's book to find which one can be used. You may wish to let the worship committee conceive and introduce to the others the idea of memorizing a scripture passage to use in worship without having to turn to the books. You may wish to have the members prepare short prayers for today's worship service.

If your juniors shared with their Sunday church schools something of what they have been doing, they may want to tell about this sharing now. There may be new pupils. Boys and girls may have had interesting experiences over the week end. You and your helpers will want to chat as friends with the juniors and learn to know them and their interests better.

Quiz Time with Panel of Leaders

Vary the quiz time this week by having a panel of four to six juniors who will be asked the questions in turn by a master of ceremonies. Individual points can be scored as the quiz progresses. Or, if the juniors were very much interested in their team's progress last week, the panel may be chosen in two parts, with the "experts" of each side allowed to consult about the answer if they wish. Keep it simple, and keep it fun. Don't allow prompting from the audience. The panel should change each day.

Introduction to the Story

Turn to the time line. Tell the juniors that many, many years had gone by since David was king. The temple had been built by his son, Solomon, who ruled in great glory. But with the death of Solomon the kingdom split in two: the Northern Kingdom, or Israel, and the Southern Kingdom, or Judah. They were never reunited. In Jesus' time the Samaritans lived and worshiped where the Northern Kingdom had been; and the people of the Southern Kingdom of Judah, or what was left of them, were known as Jews.

Many of the kings of both kingdoms were disloyal to God. The time of the story is that of a king who was being untrue not only to God, but to all his laws of justice and mercy. Dangerous as it would be for a messenger to rebuke the king and his priests and his people, God looked for a man with devotion and courage and insight to carry his message of doom to Israel.

Story

Only a Herdsman

It was hot under the blistering sun and the herds that Amos was tending were seeking every scrap of shade cast by bush or rock. The land shimmered in the heat and Amos' thoughts were far away.

He had been on a trip to the capital of the land, Samaria, the white city where the king lived. He had been on Mount Moriah where sacrifices to God were offered while singers chanted and great rams' horns were blown.

Amos' thoughts were back in Samaria and he was not happy. "They worship God," he said to himself, "but I also saw images of Kaiwan, the star god, and others. Those in high places were oppressing the poor and doing wrong to the helpless. It is not right! It is not right!"

In his mind Amos kept thinking about God, the great and holy One, and of his laws and commandments. He knew that the leaders of the land were sinning against God and against his commandments. If only there were a prophet to thunder out against this evil, and to lead the people back to God and to following God's will, Amos thought.

Then God's voice came to him as he sat under the golden heat of the sun, and the voice said, "You go, Amos. You go to Bethel, and prophesy for me. Lead my people from their wrongdoing and bring them back into loyalty to me."

Amos was aghast. "I am no prophet," he cried. "I am not even the son of a prophet. I do not know how to prophesy. I cannot speak in thundering tones of the evil that is being done against God."

But the voice of God continued to call him.

"Who am I to dare to accuse the high priest?" thought Amos. "Who am I to dare to speak out against the king? It would be as much as my life is worth."

Still the voice of God continued to call him. "Do you dare, Amos? Will you take my message to Bethel? I will give you the power to stand up before those in authority and tell them they will be destroyed if they do not mend their ways."

The days slipped by.

It was a feast day in Bethel. Great crowds were there. Offerings were being made. The smell of incense drifted on the air. Unheeded cries for justice and mercy rose from the poor and the downtrodden.

Suddenly the voice of a man rang out.

"The LORD roars from Zion,
  and utters his voice from Jerusalem;
the pastures of the shepherds mourn,
  and the top of Carmel withers."

It was a voice new to the crowd, rugged and strong, fresh and untrained to public speaking. It electrified the crowd. They fell silent and turned to see who it was that was speaking.

They saw a shepherd, a herdsman from the country, his heavy robe and head covering, his sandaled feet showing he was unaccustomed to city living. But his eyes were dark with a passionate

81

dream and his voice rose strong and unafraid. They wondered who he was, but with his next words they forgot the man and heard only the voice.

"Thus saith the LORD," he thundered. He proclaimed, one after the other, the doom of Damascus, Gaza, Tyre, Edom, and other cities inimical to the people of Israel. The crowd roared their approval. They liked to hear this kind of message from the Lord.

Amos went on, but this time he spoke of the doom of Judah. The crowd stirred uneasily. They had friends and relatives in Judah, who claimed that Judah was closer to God's way than was Israel. The man was getting too close to home.

Then it came out. Clear-cut and detailed was the accusation against Israel itself.

"They sell the righteous for silver,
and the needy for a pair of shoes—
they that trample the head of the poor into the dust of the earth,
and turn aside the way of the afflicted."

Some people muttered in anger, others lifted their heads in hope. But the priests and those in power scowled darkly. People were listening to this stranger from the country and the altars were deserted.

"Seek good and not evil,
that you may live"; proclaimed Amos.

"Hate evil and love good,
and establish justice in the gate;
it may be that the LORD, the God of hosts,
will be gracious to the remnant of Joseph."

At the end Amos proclaimed the doom of Israel and the downfall of Israel's king.

Amaziah, the high priest, could stand it no longer. He sent word to the king about this upstart prophet who dared to say such things. "It is a conspiracy against you!" he reported.

He himself spoke sternly to Amos. "Go down to Judah," he said. "Prophesy there. But stop disturbing us here. This is the king's sanctuary. This is the temple of our kingdom."

Amos replied, "It was the LORD himself who told me to come and prophesy here. You say, 'Do not preach against the house of Israel' but God says, 'You who trample upon the needy, and cheat at every observance of religion, I will destroy your temple and not one of the people shall escape alive.' "

But justice with God is ever tempered by mercy. The Book of Amos ends with the hope of salvation, with a promise of restoration and redemption of the people of Israel, of those who remain faithful and who hear the message of the Lord.

Dramatic Reading of the Story

Have the juniors turn to page 18 in their books and assign parts for reading the dramatized version of the story as told there. You may say, "We don't have any account, in the Bible, of how Amos' neighbors felt about what was happening in Bethel, but Amos must have told them how things were when he came back from his travels. Therefore, we can imagine the conversation. We can imagine, too, what people said when he spoke out for God in Bethel."

If you have basic Palestinian costumes you may use them to make the reading more real. Or you may just read the first time. Stop to let the juniors look up the Bible references and make up their own speeches at the places indicated.

This type of reading will give you opportunity for conversation about Amos, and why it took courage for him to go to Bethel. The juniors will know that kings in those days could put people in prison or kill them if they said displeasing things. Help the juniors imagine Amos confronted by the high priest. As they work out the way in which the conversation is to be rendered, they can realize better how firm and undaunted Amos was in his reply to the powerful priest.

Evaluation and Planning

This may be a good time to do some evaluation and planning. The juniors may recall what they did in the first five sessions: stories, research, reports, dramatizations (real or with puppets), making a litany, exhibits, posters, time line, choral reading, memorizing, singing, discussion, working with clay, the quiz, and other features. They may talk over and decide what helped them most to understand and enjoy the way in which the men they have been studying about responded to God's purpose for their lives. They may consider what helped them most to want to grow as able Christians themselves. They may decide, in general, whether they would like to specialize in some of these types of activity. For instance, they may be interested in the exhibit and posters. Or they may be keen about puppets. Or they may like research and reports. Or they may prefer live dramatization, making notebooks and maps. Do not give them the idea that nothing will be done except what they think they like. But let them know that what they have found most worth while will guide you in working out plans for the next four days.

Recreation

As planned by the games committee. See page 121.

Recall

When the juniors are ready, suggest that they follow out the steps of God's plan as it is shown in the Bible stories they have been studying.

They should be able to work out the following steps:

1. God planned for a people who would be his people and who would know and follow his purpose and obey his laws.

2. He chose Abraham to leave the old home and found a nation in a new land. Abraham obeyed God's call.

3. When Abraham's descendants had become very numerous and were slaves in Egypt, God planned to lead them back to the Promised Land and establish them there. Moses obeyed God's call to lead them but the people were not ready to go all the way, and had to live and learn under Moses in the wilderness.

4. After forty years they had entered the Promised Land. The tribes settled and made Canaan their home. They were ruled by judges for a long time. Then they begged God for a king and he gave them King Saul. Saul was unfaithful. But God still loved his people. He planned for David, whom he could trust, to form the tribes into a kingdom loyal to God. David built up the kingdom. He constantly tried to know God's will, repented deeply of his sins, and praised God for his goodness.

5. Solomon followed David and ruled forty years. His son Rehoboam ruled next. He was not wise. He followed bad advice instead of ruling as God's man should. The kingdom was divided. Many people were disloyal to God, although there were always some who were faithful to him. God knew that the kingdoms would be overcome by their enemies if the people and rulers continued their sinful ways. He sent Amos to try to cause them to turn to God in love and loyalty again. Amos courageously and fearlessly gave God's message to the people.

Do not try to work this out in detail. If the juniors have a general idea of God's purpose and man's response it will be enough.

Fun with Work

The juniors will probably want to put something of Amos' story into their exhibit. They may make a diorama of Amos confronting the high priest at Bethel. See Activity Sheet No. 8 for directions. If you are not using the Activity Sheets, the juniors may like to draw pictures to make a frieze telling the story. Or they may work out a dramatization from the one given in their books, either with puppets or in person.

You might suggest that the juniors learn the actual words from the Bible (see quotations on page 20 of the pupil's book) and add a scene to the playlet, in which a family or a family and friends in the city gather around and tell each other what Amos said. Such a scene would, by itself, be very appropriate for the final program. These words of Amos may likewise be woven into the worship service today. They may be brought into the conversation leading up to worship. They might also form part of the "I am . . ." dramatization or impersonation of Amos. The time line should be brought up to date. The map may have the Northern and Southern Kingdoms added, and the sites for Bethel and Jerusalem marked. The "I am . . ." impersonation for Amos may be prepared by a couple of juniors if they are interested. Quiz questions for next session may be prepared by a small committee or by all the juniors if a general quiz or panel is to use them.

Conversation

As the children gather for worship, take a few minutes to talk together as you lead up to worship for today. If you choose the theme for worship suggested below, you may wish to guide the juniors to think about problems of today. Does the kind of evil God didn't like in Bethel go on in these days? Are people being selfish and trying to get all they can for themselves? Are they living comfortably while they know others around the world are hungry and cold and sick and homeless? Guide the children to see that our world is as close to us as the little country of Palestine was to people who did not have telegraph, radio, and air travel. Is there always justice? Or do those who do wrong sometimes get off because they are rich, or because they are young, or because of some other reason? Are people doing their best to do good and to love God's way? Or are they sometimes careless about what God expects and demands, and prefer to take their own easy, comfortable way?

Worship Suggestions

The theme today may be "Seek good and not evil." Amos 5:14-15a, and 24 may be used from page 20 of the pupil's book.

The litany on page 21 of the pupil's book may be used too. A junior might be prepared to give a short talk about what he thinks Amos 5:14 can mean to boys and girls in their daily lives. You will find suitable hymns to follow such short talks among those listed on page 125 of this text.

Closing

Make any announcements that need to be made about tomorrow or the rest of the school. Commendation about co-operation or what has been accomplished would be a nice note on which to send the juniors home.

POSSIBLE STEPS IN PLANNING

First read the story of Amos in this session. Then take your Bible and read the Book of Amos. The story is not given in chronological order there, so keep in mind the story as written out. Read the suggested dramatization in the juniors' book.

Go over the suggestions for the session. Would you like to give more time to Amos? If so, read over the next session about Jeremiah. Decide whether to keep the study of Amos to one day, or to take two and be content with just telling the story of Jeremiah either in worship, or during the second day as you complete the work on Amos.

If you are going to take two days for Amos, you will need to work up a session plan which covers both days. You may take more time for some of the activities, and for discussion. You may omit the recall the first day, and use it at the beginning of the second day, including Jeremiah's story with the people going into exile because they just would not live according to God's law and purpose. Be sure your plans for both days are balanced and workable.

If you have had to put away materials and work already done at the end of session five, have some of them out, but if possible let the juniors get out and set up books, maps, Activity Sheets, to remind them of the things done last week. They enjoy digging out old treasures and will look at them with interest as they decide which to put up and which to set out.

Your helpers who are to guide the games committee should have in hand any preparation made by the committees last week. The service planned for worship today should be complete except for any parts to be chosen or carried out by juniors.

The quiz must be prepared from the questions the boys and girls made out or from those the teachers devised. Decide whether to change to a panel of experts this week. Juniors often welcome a change of form.

Prepare the introduction to the story carefully. Study your Bible dictionary, if possible, and be ready with information that will be of interest to the juniors.

Prepare the story for telling, and be ready, too, to guide the juniors to a really lively dramatic reading of the story from their books. They may want to "walk through" the action. They may want to add more scenes. A beginning scene of Amos the herdsman going through Bethel and getting cheated and seeing others cheated could be used. However, unless the juniors really want to elaborate, material in the book will give them plenty to work on.

Decide whether you want the evaluation and planning time as outlined. You may feel it wiser not to raise the question of what is best liked. Some groups become divided and disunited when the choice of a majority is adopted and the minority loses. Often an alert leader can sense without asking what is best liked and give it extra time, at the same time letting individuals do things they dearly love to do. You will, however, want to guide the pupils in some sort of evaluation.

Recall is important. We do not want to lose, in the study of these persons, the feeling that God has an overruling purpose for the welfare of his children, and that he depends on those whom he calls to help to bring that purpose about, as they devotedly answer his call to them. Plan your own method of recall, using the thoughts suggested.

Are you working at the timing? To stop before the group is tired of something, and yet to allow time for work to be finished is an art. Are you needing to do more preparation? There is no virtue in letting the juniors spend ten minutes getting materials ready and then have no time to do the work. Which is more worth while—to dress those puppets for the Amos dramatization, or to work at the dramatization with puppets with improvised costumes? Creative activity—activity which helps juniors to grow—can often take place through the use of materials already prepared.

You Shall Not Fear

This Entire Study helps us see how God gives to those whom he has chosen to do his work, the power and the courage to carry out his plans, and how, when people are willing to undertake God's work, his mighty purpose is more fully implemented in this world.

We Continue today with the story of Jeremiah, who showed steadfastness, loyalty, and courage as he answered God's call to proclaim to the faithful truths that they could hold to in the dispersion so that the faith might live forever.

The Story of Jeremiah, how he was called to serve, and how he worked to do God's will is found in the Book of Jeremiah. Specific references are: Jeremiah 1:6-9; 32:1-5; 36:1-4, 5-7, 9-10, 14*b*-19, 20-23, 24-32; 29:1-3, 5-14; 43:4-7; 44:1.

The Juniors should gain, through today's study, some knowledge of Jeremiah and the work God did through him, and an appreciation of the devotion and courage that may be needed to carry forward God's work in the world.

HIGHLIGHTS FOR THE SEVENTH SESSION

Early Arrivals:

Getting ready for the session by games and worship committees. Getting the quiz ready (the panel may be drawn from the two committees so they will not know what the questions are to be)

Class Activities:

Singing or learning a new song
Quiz Time
Introduction to the Story
Story: "Jeremiah and God's Message'
Discussion of Giving Project

Games or Other Recreation

Planning for the Next Three Days

Having Fun with Work

1. Making pictures for the time line
2. The exhibit: diorama, poster or drawings to illustrate Jeremiah's story
3. Dramatizing interview with Jeremiah with puppets, or filmstrip on Jeremiah
4. Working on dramatization or puppet play

Worship: "The Bible Is God's Word to Us"

Closing Time

PLANNING FOR THE SEVENTH DAY

This seventh day may be a continuation of the study on Amos. If so, go over the plans you made for the two days. Or this may be a session on Jeremiah. In this case, turn to "Steps in Planning," at the end of the session suggestions, and follow them. If you have used the Jeremiah story in worship the previous session (in case you are giving two sessions to Amos), you may still want to close the study of Amos with some parts of the story of Jeremiah as given in the session plan.

A POSSIBLE SEVENTH DAY SESSION

As the Juniors Come

The worship and games committees should get busy. Then another committee or all the boys and girls may work on quiz questions for the quiz panel which should be chosen from members of the two committees. If the idea of having two sides is to be used, those preparing the questions may be divided into two groups.

You may wish to begin learning "God of Grace and God of Glory" with the juniors now. It is found on the inside front cover of the pupil's book. You might say, "We have been finding out how God by his great power helped and guided the leaders he had chosen to teach, encourage, and rebuke his people. God is always pouring out his power on those who love him and who are willing to respond to his call for service, or who are willing to let their lives be guided by him. In your books there is a prayer hymn to God for help in doing what he wants us to do, and for his power to be given us. Let us turn to it and read the words and listen to the music." You will then follow your favorite and most successful way of teaching a new hymn to the juniors (see page 127 of this text for suggestions).

Juniors always enjoy picking up little jobs which need finishing. "John, could you finish this map and get it posted? It needs a little color here." Or, "Susan, we're going to be working on an interview between Jeremiah and two men of Jerusalem. Will you find three puppets to take the part, and fix a headdress for Jeremiah, like the one in this picture?"

If a committee is ready to suggest a service project, the whole class may make the choice after discussion. See page 126.

Quiz Time

Use a panel if that was decided on, or continue as fun with all taking part in two competing sides. Take time to be sure that the correct answer is explained if there is confusion about any point. Especially is this needed if questions beyond those of fact (see "Possible Steps in Planning") are being used now.

Introduction to the Story

Use these questions as an introduction. Let the juniors give brief answers. 1. God loved his people. What did he expect from them? (That they love him and want to do his will.) 2. Were they always faithful to him? (In the wilderness and from then on they were not. They kept turning aside to worship other gods.) 3. Did they follow God's good laws even when they were worshiping other gods? (No. They kept forgetting God's laws and paying no attention to what was right and good to do.) 4. What did God do when they turned away from him and began to do wrong? (He sent leaders to tell them they were wrong, and to lead them back to the right way.) 5. Can you name some of the leaders? (Moses, Nathan, Amos; the juniors may recall other prophets and teachers. If they mention Jesus, you will agree, but remind them that Jesus came to earth long after the time of the people we are studying about.) 6. You may say, "There were some good kings who loved the Lord and helped lead the people toward him. But there came a time when God knew the people would have to be carried off into captivity because they were too faithless and weakened by failure to obey God's laws. Still he sent a powerful messenger to try to win them back into right ways."

90

Story

Tell the story of Jeremiah as given below or let the juniors work it out using the procedure given on page 22 of the pupil's book. If you do the latter, you may let the juniors take turns reading what is in the text, while you read from the Bible the verses of the story as they call for them. These verses must be read smoothly and without hesitation to keep the thread of the story going.

Jeremiah and God's Message

Jeremiah, whom God had chosen to be his messenger to his people in Jerusalem, was in prison. He had been beaten and thrown into prison by the very ones who should have been listening to the counsel God was giving through the lips of his servant Jeremiah. He had been in prison for many a long day.

After a while King Zedekiah became uneasy. He didn't like to listen to God's messages, but he kept worrying. What was going to happen? Maybe Jeremiah could tell him. Maybe God had let Jeremiah know what the future held. He sent for the prisoner.

"Now tell me," whispered the king. "Is there any message from the Lord?"

"Yes," said Jeremiah sadly. "You are to be delivered into the hand of the king of Babylon." But he went on quickly. "I am only God's messenger. I have never wronged you. I have never done harm to the princes or the people. Why do you keep me in that terrible prison? If you send me back there, I'll die."

The king listened. He had a sense of justice even if he didn't often use it. "Keep him in the court of the guard," he ordered.

From there Jeremiah could get word to the people. "Don't stay in the city," he urged them. "The city is going to be taken by the Chaldeans. They will carry you into slavery, but your lives will be spared."

The things Jeremiah was saying came to the ears of some of his enemies. They complained to the princes and the princes went to the king.

"He deserves to be put to death. He's taking all the heart out of the defense," they stormed. "Even the soldiers are wondering if they should continue to defend the city."

The king knew that Jeremiah was right. Nothing could save the city. If the people left, their lives would be saved.

But he was afraid of the princes. "Do anything you want to do to Jeremiah," he said. "I wouldn't dream of opposing your wishes."

There was an old cistern in the court of the guard. It had no water in it, but there was filthy mud, almost deep enough to cover a person.

"We won't kill him outright," they said. "We'll let him down into the well gently, with ropes. Then he'll get weaker and weaker. Will it be our fault if he sinks into the mud and dies?"

They brought the ropes and let Jeremiah down into the well.

He stood up, leaning against the wall. He must stand up just as long as he could. For when his muscles

91

gave way and he sank down, the mud would cover his head and he would die.

All over the court the whisper ran. "They've put Jeremiah into the old cistern. Do you think they'll let him die there?"

In the king's house was an Ethiopian, who was a friend of Jeremiah's. The whisper came to him. He looked around for the king.

But the king was not there. He was sitting in the Benjamin Gate.

"I'll have to find him," said Ebed-melech, the Ethiopian. "I cannot let Jeremiah perish."

He went to the king.

"Those men who threw Jeremiah the prophet into the cistern did what was evil," he said to the king, boldly. "You know he'll die there of hunger."

The king looked uneasy. He could ignore what he didn't know about, but to know and do nothing would be to be responsible for Jeremiah's death.

"Take three of my men, and get Jeremiah out of the cistern," he said to Ebed-melech.

The Ethiopian hurried to use his permission. It wasn't going to be easy to pull Jeremiah out of the mud. He thought a minute.

Then he went to the storehouse and got some old garments and rags. He got a rope. He went to the court of the guard.

"I'm letting rope down, Jeremiah," he said, "and some old clothing. Put it under your armpits before you put the rope under them. Then we'll try to get you out of that mud."

Jeremiah must have breathed a quick prayer of thanks to God. Now he would be able to go on with the work of his life, the carrying of God's message to his people.

He padded his armpits with the old cloths. He settled the ropes. Then the four men pulled, slowly but firmly. Jeremiah wriggled and twisted. The mud was almost like quicksand. But at last his body came free. He was hauled to the surface.

Jeremiah bathed and put on clean garments. He ate. Then he was ready to take up his work. Although he was still a prisoner in the court of the guard, his life was safe, and he could speak to the people.

Jerusalem was taken. Zedekiah was blinded and taken prisoner to Babylon.

Jeremiah was rescued from the court of the guard by the soldiers of the king of Babylon, and allowed to go home in peace. God had used him to give to the people truths that they could carry away into captivity with them. Even in far lands they would be able to be faithful to God and to know what his will for them was.

Jeremiah lived on in Judah for a while. Then the people who were left distrusted God again. They fled to Egypt and took Jeremiah with them. God did not desert his rebellious people. He spoke to them through Jeremiah's messages.

Discussion of Giving Project

If those who came first worked with you on a plan for a giving project (see "Possible Steps in Planning"), have them present it; or you may say, "Jeremiah set down God's message to the people. The king destroyed it. So he patiently made another copy. God's word must reach people. We can have a part in sharing God's word with others. We can help to send his Word where it is not known or where copies of it have been lost or destroyed by fire, earthquake, flood, or war."

The juniors may discuss what they would like to do about this and work out a plan to bring gifts for the purpose on the next three days. (See suggestions on page 126.)

Games

As planned by the games committee. See p. 122.

Planning for the Next Three Days

If there is to be an exhibit and a program for parents and friends on the last day of the school, definite plans should be made now for exactly what will be presented, and who will do it. If the exhibit is to include all the work done, the items to be displayed may be considered. If no program is planned, it will still be worth while to plan together for a recall program for the group itself, with perhaps some voting on what "I like best" among the things done. Perhaps one guest, someone very special, can be counted on to be present to add the pleasure of getting ready for some other person's enjoyment and approval.

Having Fun with Work

More pictures may be made for the time line. Sometimes boys and girls like to make pictures of Bible characters and you can help them find the right place in the time line for each picture.

Parts of Jeremiah's story may be worked out in some form. Diorama, puppet show, poster using the figures from Activity Sheet No. 7, an interview with Jeremiah done with puppets or as a "live" show, drawings, or impersonation of Jeremiah or Barach may be done. (Barach might come back to Jeremiah and tell Jeremiah what happened in the king's palace.)

If the story of Amos is being dramatized, work will need to be done on that.

A small group might work on quiz questions for tomorrow.

Worship Suggestions

Perhaps for today the theme, "The Bible Is God's Word to Us," might be used. The responsive statement given on page 124 of this text might be given by the adult leader with the committee responding. A hymn of praise, such as "God of Grace and God of Glory," inside front cover of the pupil's book may be used. The adult leader might give a short talk about what the Bible has meant in the lives of people of today and what it can mean to us. A longer story could be taken from *Stories of the Book of Books,* if you have it. You might like to adapt the "Litany of Praise" on page 21 of the pupil's book, to bring in thanks to God for the Bible. (Since the pupils all make the same response, they do not need their books for this and the leader can use any phrases that fit into the thought for today.) "The Word of God Shall Be My Guide," or any other similar hymn may be used following the talk.

Evaluation

A very brief evaluation time may follow worship today. You may ask, "Do you remember the day we started our study with finding out how God chose Abraham to begin a task that was to go on down through the centuries? What would you say has happened when men like Abraham and Moses and David and Amos and Jeremiah have been willing to let God guide them and fit them to do what he wanted done?" (The juniors should be able to give some such results as: First families and then a nation grew up in which there were people devoted to and loyal to God even when others forgot his ways. People came to understand more and more clearly what God wants people to do and think and be. God was able to have a people who even in exile could be true to him.) "In what ways did the men we have been studying about show that they were letting God use their lives?" (The juniors may mention such things as Amos' fearlessness, Abraham's devotion, Moses' earnest attention to God's laws, Jeremiah's determination to let nothing hinder his giving of God's message to the people, David's wholeheartedness in trying to do what God wished, and his repentance when he himself did what was wrong.) "How does God help us know today what he wants for our lives?" (The juniors may think of points that have been brought up in the study so far: the Bible, teachers, and God's guidance in our hearts.) You may want to have the children think about gains in learning to live more happily with others, being kinder, more loving, and more helpful, if such has been the case.

Closing Time

Recall briefly what is planned for the next three days and make any assignments for special duties which are to be undertaken tomorrow in preparation.

POSSIBLE STEPS IN PLANNING

For this seventh day you are either continuing with the study of Amos, or you are taking a look at Jeremiah and his patient perseverance in giving God's message to the people. In any case read through the session procedures suggested for today, since you may want to pick up some of them in planning for your last day.

Read the story of Jeremiah as given in the pupil's book looking up the scripture references and reading them carefully. Think about Jeremiah's life of patient service. If possible read in your Bible dictionary about him. If he is real to you, you will make him real to the juniors.

Decide how the quiz is to be handled. If a panel is to be used, it could be made up of members of the games or worship committee so that the rest can get the questions ready. However, you may prefer to have other juniors on the panel, and complete the questions yourself. Questions by now should include such things as: Why didn't David kill Saul when he could have? (Because he refused to kill anyone whom God had anointed king.) Knowing the facts of the Bible story is not enough. The juniors need to know what God's purpose was and how men responded to God's love and will.

How is worship developing? Are the juniors more able to worship meaningfully? Can they prepare adequately with the help of an adult? Are they better able to take part? You may need to be giving more thought to the service of worship and preparation for it.

Is the recreation truly a time of refreshment and enjoyment? Is there variety? Are the juniors learning something new? Are they improving in their play relationships? Do not neglect games as a time for developing as joyous Christians.

Most vacation church schools want to have a project for giving. One related to the spread of the scriptures is appropriate and would rise naturally from this lesson. See "Giving Projects" in the Appendix page 126. Several of the juniors may look at any material you have on various projects and choose one to recommend, or you may tell very briefly about the one which you feel will be best undertaken and then let the juniors decide whether, and what, to do about it.

Prepare very carefully the introduction to the story and the story itself. Decide whether to use the study-it-out form in the pupil's book, or the story furnished in this book.

As usual, you will need to know just what state your work enterprises are in. Abandon any to which the juniors must be driven. Stress those which they are enjoying, and find ways to relate them more and more closely to the thought of how men of courage rose in answer to God's call to help carry out his purpose. Often a title for a poster, or a card of explanation for a diorama will give this point to what otherwise is just busy work.

Memory work will likely be incidental but none the less carefully planned. It may come in worship as the juniors use a passage they have been learning. A few minutes of worship preparation *before worship begins* might be needed for the recall of the passage to be used today. Making a poster for all to use in worship or in a final program will help those who prepare it learn the words of any passage the juniors have chosen to learn.

Be sure materials are on hand for the various kinds of work. With younger juniors it is often better for the teacher to decide on something they can do effectively than to let them choose from a large number of activities which they are not yet capable of carrying out. Or a simple, "Would you like to make a table-top scene or a diorama?" may give them a limited choice.

Your notebook for this seventh day should carry *your* plan, with references to the pages in this text to which you need to turn for exact instructions.

Firm as a Rock!

This Entire Study guides us to realize how God chooses and uses those who are willing to do his will, and to carry out his mighty purposes. It helps us know how he gives them strength and courage and whatever is needed to accomplish the task that he has set for them.

We Continue Today with the story of Peter, a rash, brash man, who failed one test, and yet whom Jesus later compared to a rock. We watch him become firm as a rock as he devotes his life and his will in response to God's call.

The Story of Peter is found in the Gospels and in the first part of Acts. Specifically you may use: Mark 1:16, 18; 9:2-8; Matthew 16:13-20; John 13:36-38; 18:25-27; Luke 22:59-62; John 21:15-17; Acts 2:14, 22-24, 32; 3:1-15; 4:1-5, 5-13, 19-20; 5:40-42; 10; 15:6-11.

The Juniors should come to realize how the power of God, through Jesus Christ and the Holy Spirit, entered into Peter's life and changed him from an unstable follower to one whom God could use in building the church.

HIGHLIGHTS FOR THE EIGHTH SESSION

Early Arrivals: Singing, browsing, finishing up, preparing parts for today's session.

Class Activity:

Quiz Time
Introduction to the Story
Story: "Firm as a Rock"
Committee Reports on Plans for the Final Session

Recreation

Having Fun with Work

1. Making a frieze of Peter's life
2. Adding to time line

3. Looking at exhibit of completed projects
4. Enjoying dramatics (puppets, live shows, interviews)
5. Continuing Bible study
6. Making a scroll with Peter's quotation from the Psalms

Worship: "God's Love for the World"
Closing Time

PLANNING FOR THE EIGHTH DAY

Examine suggested plans for this and the ninth and tenth days. Estimate time that is left carefully. After going over the procedures suggested below, turn to "Possible Steps in Planning," on page 102 and work out your own session plans in your notebook, fitting them to your situation.

A POSSIBLE EIGHTH-DAY SESSION

As the Juniors Come

If it was decided to take an offering, you may want to gather it now, rather than have the juniors carry money about till worship time. Or they may keep it till time for worship and put it in the offering plate.

Worship and games committees will meet to complete their plans. Plans may allow a little time for the juniors to practice reading scripture, or learning a hymn, or preparing some recreation equipment if they wish. A committee for the last day should be set up if this has not been done, and with the help of a teacher should plan details. You may want to use all the juniors not in the games or worship committees, but most groups will prefer a small committee. If the juniors are still enjoying thinking up questions to "stump" the experts, they may work at that. You might be wise to have questions ready in case they do not wish to work at this. Juniors often get suddenly tired of preparation work they have enjoyed previously. Individual children often like to pick up odds and ends of work to finish as they come in. New books and pictures of New Testament times should be added to references. They are needed to introduce Peter and Paul.

Quiz Time

Have a panel or the two groups as has been decided. Keep it fun. By now you should be able to "spring" questions from the earlier quizzes which will help in recall.

Introduction to the Story

Using the time line and your Bible, point out that in our study we have come to the end of the Old Testament story. About 400 years went by between the last events of the Old Testament and the times of the New Testament. You may go on to say, "God had sent teacher after teacher to his people, and still many didn't understand him or realize what he really wanted them to do. Of the few who did, many refused to follow God's way. So at last he sent his Son, our Lord Jesus, to save his people.

"Jesus, you remember, chose twelve men to be his disciples and to learn from him.

"But just as they had rejected the great teachers and prophets, the leaders of the Jews rejected the Son of God. They crucified him. Jesus' earthly life and service were over. But death could not hold our Lord, and he rose from the dead and walked and talked with his disciples.

"One had betrayed him, but was now dead. One had denied him. That one was Peter. Jesus had changed Peter's name at one time. He had named him Cephas which means *rock*. Peter is the Greek for *rock*. What sort of a rock was Peter going to be? Could God depend on him? He had been a coward. Would he become brave?"

Story

Use the story from page 25 of the pupil's book. Or you may prefer to have the story developed through Bible study as follows, having groups of two or three study together. When the study is over, the juniors will gather, and you will ask the questions and let the answers be given by the person or group who have just learned them. You may want to summarize the story by giving briefly what is found in the pupil's book.

Directed Bible Study

THE STORY OF PETER

What kind of work did Peter do? (Mark 1:16-18.) Notice that he was called Simon in those days.

Which disciple first acknowledged Jesus as the Christ? Matthew 16:13-20.

Which disciple declared he would lay down his life for Jesus? John 13:36-38.

Was Peter always loyal to Jesus? John 18:25-27.

How did Peter feel, after denying his Lord? Luke 22:59-62.

After the resurrection Jesus met Peter and the others by the sea of Galilee. Did Jesus forgive Peter for that denial? John 21:15-17.

How was Peter to show that he really loved Jesus? Did Peter begin to speak out boldly for Christ? Acts 2:14, 22-24, 32, 36.

Did it get Peter into trouble? Acts 3:1-15; 4:1-3.

How did Peter speak to the rulers? Acts 4:5-13.

How did Peter answer their order never to preach about Jesus again? Acts 4:19-20.

Did Peter have to suffer because of his courage? Acts 5:40-42.

Did Peter follow God's leading about what he was to do? Acts 10:1-48.

Did Peter help Paul open the church to the Gentiles? Acts 15:6-11.

To close you may say, "Peter never again denied his Lord. He was a leader in the church and he was true till the end of his life. No one really knows how he died but he is supposed to have been crucified in Rome, still faithful to his Lord and Savior."

Conversation and Evaluation

In an informal conversation guide the juniors to evaluate what they have considered so far in the study. They will recall that God has a great purpose for mankind and that he chose one person after another to reveal through them his will for people. Our Lord Jesus was his greatest gift to the world. They may come to-day to the conclusion that of all Jesus' apostles Peter was the one who most boldly proclaimed Jesus' death and resurrection as part of the plan and purpose of God. Guide the conversation to bring out the fact that God used Peter to help establish the church on a firm foundation, and to extend the good news to the Gentiles as well as the Jews.

Ask the juniors to turn to page 6 of the pupil's book and read there words from the Old Testament that Peter felt so important that he quoted them in his letter. The juniors may read the words over again, or say them together if they learned them. They may think of what these teachings perhaps meant in the life of a child of Peter's day; of what they could mean in the lives of all of us today if we pay attention to them.

Committee Reports on Last-Day Plans

The games committee should report any special plans for the next two days, or for today's recreation. The worship committee should be ready to report and ask co-operation in preparing for worship for the last day. The committee for last-day activities may announce what the procedures will be, whether they be short, or take up most of the time. If plans can be organized now, it will help.

Recreation

As planned by the games committee.

Having Fun with Work

Information about Peter should be entered on the time line with whatever device is being used.

A scroll with Peter's quotation from the Old Testament, from page 6 of the pupil's book, may be made by each junior, or by the group as a sample for the exhibit.

"I am Peter," a first-person telling by Peter of highlights of his life may be worked out. Or a puppet interview with Peter may be developed.

Work on dramatizations may continue or if any group is prepared, it may perform for the entire group.

Exhibits may be prepared if that is in the plan for the last day.

Worship

Worship today should be a high point of the session. It may come, if convenient, right after the conversation, preceding the games. A possible theme is: "God's Love for the World." The call to worship might be Isaiah 55:6-7, or 1 Chronicles 16:23-24 from page 6 of the pupil's book, especially if the juniors have learned it by heart. "God of Grace and God of Glory," would be a good opening hymn. A short talk may stress God's love for the world in sending Jesus, using John 3:16, and relating it to the outgoing of those who loved and believed in Jesus to carry the news of salvation to the ends of the earth. The litany on page 21 of the pupil's book may be adapted by the worship leader into a litany of thanks for the coming of Jesus and of his embodiment of God's love for us. "Lord, I Want to Be a Christian in My Heart," would be a suitable hymn.

Closing Moments

You may wish to say that tomorrow the study will be about a man who had incredible adventures as he gave his life to doing God's will, and carrying the gospel message near and far. Ask boys and girls to think of some ways to share the events of the school with their parents.

POSSIBLE STEPS IN PLANNING

Your notebook will be needed as you lay out plans for this eighth day. You will find it wise to outline your plans for the ninth and tenth days as well, so that you can assign items to the day where they will fit in best.

This is the moment when suggestions in this text, even if you have been following it fairly closely, need to be cut to your own pattern of need.

Have the juniors prepared dramatizations? Perhaps it is more important to have time to present the dramatizations than to try to do much committee work as the boys and girls arrive. Perhaps your helpers need to take over game preparation while the pupils enjoy the various dramatic presentations, live or puppet, which have been prepared. If dramatizations grew out of the study as they should have, they will form an excellent recall at the beginning of today's session and clear the way for the study of God's will as carried forward by Peter and by Paul. You may want to omit the quiz.

Plan carefully for the transition statement before coming to Peter. Use something like the one given under "Introduction to the Story," or something quite different. But make the point clear.

If at all possible, have the juniors themselves tell the story of Peter. It is given in the pupil's book in language and in short incidents easy for juniors to present. If you do it yourself, weave it into one story. With older juniors you may want to have a guided study on Peter instead, using the material in this book, letting the juniors study it and then tell what they have found out about

Peter. In any case follow the story with a little discussion, to help the juniors see that Peter, as his loyalty and devotion to Christ deepened and as he saw God's purpose in sending Jesus to be the Savior of the world, was able to overcome his shrinking from danger, and to face anything at all, for the sake of proclaiming God's love as shown in the coming of Jesus.

Think about the need for reports. Perhaps things are working out so that they are not needed. Perhaps you can simply have a chart posted and list on it last-day procedures as they are ready. One problem is to have time enough. Don't spend it in unnecessary reports. But if the reports are valuable for the juniors' growth in responsibility, make a place for them.

Today you may want to help the juniors enjoy the beautiful, rhythmic voicing of the scripture passages as they recall those they have learned, or you may want to guide the juniors to interpret Peter's quotation from Psalm 34:12-15 (page 6 in the pupil's book), learning to appreciate it, read it well, and apply it to their own lives.

If a new dramatization for live or puppet presentation seems desirable, the two contrasting scenes, Peter's denial and Peter's steadfastness before the council, would work up into good thought-provoking drama, and they are simple enough for the juniors to plan them themselves by using the scripture accounts together with what is given in their books.

Think over the various ways suggested for the inclusion of Peter in the time line, in dioramas, and in pictures.

Study the words from 1 Peter on page 6 of the pupil's book, and consider ways in which you may use the ideas given here to help juniors with their problems in their daily lives. The selection is a quotation from Psalms, so do not attribute this teaching to Peter himself.

Be sure you have all materials and implements that you will need where they can be easily reached. Does your work area need tidying or reorganization? Is more space needed for pinning up posters and pictures? A length of cloth can often be stretched to provide "pin-up" space. An old sheet torn in two and dipped in cold water dye of a suitable color makes a good background.

Not Your Way But My Way

This Entire Study guides us to see that mankind must go in God's way if his great purposes are to be accomplished, and that man's will must come into harmony with God's will if man is to live at his highest and best.

We Continue Today with the story of Paul who thought he was serving God in his own way but who was led by God to see how wrong he was; and with the account of the tremendous effect of his life of adventure and devotion in the true service of God as he took the message of salvation through Christ into faraway places.

The Story of Paul is found in the Book of Acts beginning with Acts 7:58. The letters which he wrote to the churches and to his friends contain his message and much of his firsthand experience. For parts of the story read Acts 7:58—8:1; 9:1-30; 16:11-40; 17:16-18; 19:21—20:1; 27:1—28:10.

Through This Study, the juniors should come to admire Paul and to grow in desire to live as Christians; to help send the gospel message to those who do not have it, and to support the great cause of Christ in the church.

HIGHLIGHTS FOR THE NINTH SESSION

Early Arrivals: Getting ready for the session in worship, games, and last-day committees

Singing and browsing through books, maps, and completed projects

Class Activities:

Quiz Time

Introduction to Paul

Story: "The Story of Paul"

Recall of Previous Sessions and Evaluation

Bible Study: Paul's message

Recreation

Plans for Next Session. (This will include planning how to share with parents.)

Having Fun with Work
1. Completing the time line
2. Making a litany
3. Working on the Exhibit
4. Practicing dramatization (puppets, live, interview, letter from Paul)
5. Rehearsing for the last session
6. Conversation and summary

Worship: "God and His World"

Closing Time

PLANNING FOR THE NINTH DAY

In planning for the ninth session much depends on your plans for the tenth day. If it is to be a guest day, you will need to do a great deal of recall today as you get ready for the program. If you are to have just one guest and a summary of conclusions for your study, more time can be given to thinking about Paul and how he gave himself to the task that God set for him. See the "Possible Steps in Planning," given after the session suggestions.

A POSSIBLE NINTH-DAY SESSION

As the Juniors Come

Follow your usual procedure, giving, if possible, extra time to music. The juniors may perfect something they will use in worship today or tomorrow. If there are to be guests at the last session, pupils may begin to set up the exhibit of work done and make notes about unfinished bits. Or they may make explanatory cards to go with the exhibits.

Quiz Time

This will be the last time for a class-planned quiz, and in the last session you will use the second quiz from Activity Sheet No. 2 if you are using the sheets. You may tell the juniors that a paper and pencil quiz similar to the one they took at the beginning will be used tomorrow. "It will be fun to see how much more you can tell about the men we studied than you could on our first day together."

Introduction to Paul

Have a brief recall. Some of the juniors will remember something about Paul. Perhaps you may note on a chalkboard in a word or two the things they remember, putting them more or less under three headings: *At First; Paul's Adventures; Paul's Teachings.* Have the juniors turn to Acts 9:10-16 and read it. You may say, "Paul began as an enemy of the Christians. But God planned to use his wisdom, courage, and strength, to establish the church in far lands. Would Paul be able to do all that God wanted him to do? Let's find out more about Paul."

Report

Let a junior report on the Roman Empire and how it made possible the journeys of Paul as he carried the gospel to many lands. The material will be found on page 28 of the pupil's book. Or you may have the juniors turn to their books and take turns giving the statements there.

Story

Just how you will handle the story of Paul will depend on how much your juniors know about him. If there are even a few children who seem not to know anything of Paul, tell the story more or less as it is given in the pupil's book. Or, if you prefer, and your juniors like the method, use the questions and answers given below, guiding them to recall the answer, or giving them the answer if they do not readily recall it. If your juniors do know about Paul, you may instead take one of the stories of his courage and steadfastness right from the Bible and go into it in detail. Suitable passages to choose from are: Acts 16:11-40; 19:21—20:1; 27:1—28:10.

THE STORY OF PAUL

Here are some questions and answers which can be used as such, or can be used as information to build up a story that you can tell.

What do you know about Paul's boyhood?

He was born in Tarsus, in Cilicia, of a Jewish family which had Roman citizenship. He was brought up very strictly. There were other members of his family who were influential. His sister, later on, lived in Jerusalem. As he grew older, Paul, who was called Saul among Jewish people, went to Jerusalem. He studied with the great teacher Gamaliel, and he became one of the very strictest of the Pharisees.

How did Paul act toward the Christians?

At first Paul thought they were all wrong. He thought that Jesus was just a misled teacher who was rightly put to death. He felt that all those who were spreading what he thought were lies about the resurrection of Jesus should be arrested. He felt they should even be put to death as false teachers. He believed that he was serving God in persecuting the Christians. He worked so hard at it that the Christians even far away in Damascus had heard of him and were afraid of him. But God brought about a great change in Paul.

Why did Paul become a Christian?

Paul was on his way to Damascus to arrest Christians and drag them in chains to Jerusalem. On the road a strong blinding light struck him and Jesus himself spoke to him. Paul was blinded when he got to his feet. He was led to Damascus by his traveling companions and for three days he sat in darkness and tried to think of the meaning of what had happened. God led him to realize that Jesus was indeed the Son of God, the Christ, the Savior of his people, and that the Christians had been right and he had been wrong. When God sent one of the Damascus Christians to him, Paul was ready to be baptized and to begin preaching powerfully the message of Jesus.

Were the Christians still afraid of Paul?

Yes, they were. When he came to Jerusalem, the Christians thought he was using a trick to get into their meetings so he would know which ones were Christians. But Barnabas, a generous-hearted Christian, heard what Paul had to say, and brought him to the rest.

Did anyone persecute Paul?

From the very beginning he was often in danger. Friends had to let him down from the Damascus wall at night to save him from the anger of the Jewish leaders there. They had to send him away from Jerusalem back to his old Tarsus home to save his life in Jerusalem. After he began his wonderful missionary journeys, he was often attacked, beaten, thrown into prison, stoned, or left for dead. But nothing could stop him from telling others of his faith in our Lord Jesus.

What were some of those travels?

He made three missionary journeys. Each time he went further, and to new places. He may have made a fourth journey. Old, old documents written early in the Christian years, say he went to Spain after his first imprisonment in Rome, and before his second imprisonment and death.

Did Paul have adventures?

As we read it, one adventure seemed to follow another. But there were weeks and months and years of quiet work in between when he stayed in one place or another, being used by God to build up the church. He usually worked at the trade he had been taught as a boy, that of tentmaking. But on the Lord's day and in the evenings, and to those who came around as he worked, he was able to talk about his Lord Jesus and what being a Christian meant.

Tell about one adventure

Tell the incident from Lystra from page 30 of the pupil's book.

Tell the incident about being imprisoned and the earthquake from page 31 of the pupil's book.

Tell us just one more story

Tell the incident from Ephesus from page 31 of the pupil's book.

What happened to Paul in the end?

Paul came back to Jerusalem. He was arrested on a false charge. The Romans rescued him but they didn't free him. At last he asked to be sent to Rome to Caesar for judgment. After an adventurous journey he reached there and was allowed to rent a house to live in. He lived in that house for two years but he was chained day and night to a Roman soldier. There he wrote and preached and taught and visited with people. We think he was freed after that, and was able to travel again for a while preaching and teaching, but in the end he was condemned while in prison in Rome and because he was a Roman citizen was put to death by the sword, rather than in another way.

(One interesting way to use this form of the story is for one or two helpers to sit with the storyteller, and ask the questions. The storyteller would reply in her own words, giving the thoughts supplied above as her answer. If this is done, the storyteller should not enlarge on the accounts. Keep them short. Otherwise the question-answer interest is lost.)

Recall and Evaluation

You may want to recall from the past sessions how God gave seemingly impossible tasks to men whom he chose because he knew they *could* carry his purpose forward. The juniors may mention what it was God wanted done by each man, and how that man measured up to God's trust in him. Be sure to guide the conversation so that each junior has a chance to consider what he gained from the study. Has each gained a growing understanding of the fact that whether our abilities be great or small, God has a purpose for our lives if we yield to his guidance; that we can mean much to the accomplishment of God's purpose as we live lives that are our loving response to God's love and purpose for us?

Studying God's Message as Given by Paul

Have the children turn to page 24 in their books and follow the study "When the Bible Speaks to Us," which guides them in one way of opening their hearts to God's guidance. It is appropriate to use the passage from Paul's writings since you have studied them. They may be guided, too, to imagine this message as being received by the people of the church at Corinth, and of their thinking about how it could affect their actions toward each other.

This study and consideration may lead to the juniors wanting to make a wall hanging, or poster or illuminated card with these words on it. Or you may put other words of Paul into language that someone speaking today would use, thinking about what guidance God has to give us through these words. Some suitable verses for such study will be found in Philippians 4:8; Colossians 3:20, 23; 1 Thessalonians 5:12-18, 21-22; 1 Corinthians 10:23-24; Romans 12:9-18; Hebrews 12:2-14.

Recreation

As arranged by the committee.

Plans for the Final Session

If you are having guests and a program, plans should be laid out clearly, with each junior's duties clearly outlined. Some of the work time may be used for specific preparation.

Dramatization

If planning is not necessary, take time now for one or more of the dramatizations that has been prepared for presentation. If a play about Peter was prepared yesterday, use this opportunity to let everyone see and comment on it.

Having Fun with Work

What is done in this session depends entirely on your plans.

First order of the day may be preparation for the program tomorrow, if guests are expected. This may not take too much time if good preparation has been made along the way.

Pictures from Paul's life may be added to the time line. Scenes from Paul's life may be added to the exhibit. Consult the New Testament sections of the Bible atlases.

A dramatic possibility, which will not take much time to work out, would be for the juniors to represent the people of the church at Corinth, and have a messenger come with a letter from Paul. One member may read aloud the passage from 1 Corinthians, Chapter 13 and suggest that they all learn it. He could read it phrase by phrase and have each phrase repeated by all the members. They could then comment about how they think Paul's message will help them. Costumes help such a dramatization. Often just a headdress is enough in very informal conversation with each other. Imaginative play will give room for the juniors to tell what they think about Paul and of God's purpose for his life.

If you need an extra activity, let the juniors make a litany, thanking God for the people of Bible times about whom they have studied. (See Appendix page 128 for guidance in making litanies.) Or use a form something like this:

For Abraham who with great faith left his home to go where
    you wanted him to go,
We thank you, O Lord.
For Moses who . . .
We thank you, O Lord.

The litany would be a sort of recall, helping the juniors see men as being called of God and having the courage to go out to do what God wanted them to do.

Conversation

You may wish to have a brief conversation, guiding the juniors to consider to what extent they have fulfilled the purpose of the course. Have they come to know more of God's purpose for his world as they have found out how he worked through his chosen instruments, the men of faith and loyalty and courage? Have they learned how these men grew under God's guidance more able to do for God's people what he wanted done? Do they understand that God is able to give each of us today the guidance to do his will and to respond to him in love, faith, loyalty, and service?

Worship Suggestions

The theme for today may be "God and His World." You may select hymns and scripture from the pupil's book and use the litany made today. Or use the litany given in the pupil's books.

You will perhaps want to speak briefly of the greatness and goodness of God, who, having created the universe, magnificent and beyond our understanding, created man to be his own child, and to grow in love and understanding of him, to do his will in loving response. You will want to speak of the greatness of God's love which forgives our wrongdoing when we repent of it. If an offering is to be dedicated, plan carefully for that. See the section "Worshiping Together" on page 123 for other suggestions.

111

Closing Moments

Any announcements about the next session should be made clearly now.

POSSIBLE STEPS IN PLANNING

This ninth day must be planned very carefully. You probably have three things to keep in mind: recall; thinking about Paul; and tomorrow's program. You must ask yourself two questions: What can we accomplish on this ninth day that will mean most to the juniors? What can we accomplish on the tenth day?

Put down first, exactly what *must* occur, that is, what will mean most to the Christian growth of your juniors on each of these two days. (Remember that learning facts is not necessarily growth. Accomplishing a program which truly reflects what the pupils have been thinking about may mean more than learning more facts.) Be realistic. Make a timetable. You may find that there is a half hour tomorrow which can be used easily for completing some one bit of preparation. It can be omitted then, today, thus easing today's schedule.

Sometimes, at the end of a course, it becomes wise to cut out something that had been planned because it just cannot be done without jeopardizing everything else. You may, in the session, want to let the boys and girls vote on whether or not to omit something. Facing the need to do so, may spur them to decide to work harder and accomplish more.

Keep in mind that this is a *joyful* experience for you and for the boys and girls. It is fun. It is exciting to see ideas take shape and form. Juniors delight in watching each other take part. Amusing incidents often occur. Approach the last two sessions with a light and merry heart. This is preparation as much as making time schedules.

Go over all the suggestions. Arrange your very own program for today's session, keeping as much flexibility as possible so that juniors may share in planning and help make decisions.

Take stock. Know exactly how you will introduce each item. How will you enlist the junior's interest? Can you give leadership responsibilities to certain ones, guide others in making explanatory cards for the exhibit items, or lead in lining up the rest for singing or work on scriptures? Note their names. Be sure

112

that you do not choose people already assigned to other committee work.

Consider ways to share the events of the school with parents. If the pupils have already planned a program, you may invite a guest to show slides on travel in Bible lands to climax the event.

Decide whether or not to have the quiz. If you do, be sure the questions are ready and your panel members noted so you need not hesitate in announcing who has been chosen for that. Determine when you will make the announcement about the quiz for tomorrow.

Plan your introduction to Paul. You may want to have a junior prepared ahead of time to read the scripture passage. Another junior or one of your helpers should be ready with a report from the pupil's book on the Roman Empire. Decide on which suggestion you will use for the story of Paul and make your preparation in accordance with your decision.

Study very carefully the suggestions for fun with work. Again, what you choose will depend largely on what you have already done and what is planned for tomorrow. The litany, if prepared, could be used in worship in the next session, and would help guests to get a feeling of the entire study.

The Kingdom . . . . Shall Become

This Entire Study helps us realize that God has a mighty purpose for this world of his, and that he has, down through the ages, chosen men of loyalty and devotion to work toward the time when the kingdom of the world may become "the kingdom of our Lord and of his Christ, and he shall reign for ever and ever." It helps us see that those who answer God's call to service in his name are given strength and power and wisdom and patience to do what God purposes that they shall do.

Today we gather together the threads of the study and think further about what God's purpose demands in our lives. We recall many things that we have studied during these ten sessions.

Scripture for Today will be taken from selections studied in previous sessions.

PLAN I

Highlights for the Tenth Session (with guests present)

Early Arrivals: Getting ready for the session by arranging the room, working on exhibit and other committees, preparing for guests.

Class Activities:

Written quiz
Program for the guests, including
Worship: "Giving Praise to God"

Recreation in which the guests join, viewing filmstrip and slides on Bible lands

Getting ready to take things home

Dismissal

PLAN II

Highlights for the Tenth Session (no guests present)

Early arrivals: Arranging the room, working on committees, reviewing pupil's book, studying the Bible, using references.

Class Activities:

Recall Planned by the Juniors

Recreation

A Program for Ourselves

Conducted Tour of the Exhibit

Worship: "Giving Praise to God"

Getting Ready to Take Things Home

Dismissal

PLANNING FOR THE TENTH DAY

You and your pupils and helpers have already made most of the plans for today, and your notebook has in it a time schedule for what is to take place. But there is still the detail to work out in relation to your plans for the last session. The day should move smoothly. Juniors should do just as much of the presentation as possible. More detailed suggestions for planning are given after the next section.

A POSSIBLE TENTH-DAY SESSION

If you are going to have a program for guests, you have probably planned for four main parts of the session. First, the final preparations that the juniors must make as they arrive, and for a limited time thereafter. Second, the quiz which you announced at the last session, using the second part of the Activity Sheet No. 2, if you are using the sheets. Third, the greeting of guests and the presentation of the program. It may include information, dramatization, memory work, reports, a tour of the exhibit, choral reading, music, worship, and games. Fourth, after the program while guests are visiting, each junior will want to gather up the things he is going to take home. This should include clay tablets, figures, scenes, posters, worship books, the sheets from the activity packets, if you have used them, the pupil's books, and anything else that can be distributed. You may let such things as the big map be chosen by some junior who would like to put it up on his wall at home. Puppets, especially, will be valuable for recall at home.

You will want to call the group together, perhaps, at the end for a last song, and a friendly good-by with thank you's to anyone who has been a special helper.

If you are not having a program for guests you may follow some such plan as this:

As the Juniors Come

Let each set up his work in the exhibit for the guided tour later on. Committees may meet if they are needed, and individual juniors may finish up bits of work that they did not get done.

Even though there are no guests, they are going to have a program for themselves.

Written Quiz

Using Activity Sheet No. 2, if you have it, give the two quizzes for the end of the study. When the juniors have finished them, you may have a bit of conversation, giving them the correct answers. Some groups like to trade papers and let the juniors correct each others' papers with a bright-colored crayon or pencil while you give the correct answers. Keep the quiz informal, but be sure that the juniors get the correct information.

Recall

This may be a lively part of the session, as you all sit in a circle (double circle if necessary), and you designate juniors here and there to recall spontaneously parts of the study. "Who will tell us how it happened that Abraham left his home and traveled with all his family, his flocks and herds and servants and fighting men, to a new land?" (Jimmy does so.) "Did it take courage?" (Comments from the group.) "God had in mind a wonderful purpose for the world which he had made. He intended the world with all its devotion to things that are not good or right to become in the end his own kingdom, where men would live as children of God and follow his great purposes. Abraham's family was led to start a people, and later to become a nation, who would follow in God's way. Now tell me, Louise, something about Moses." (Louise will be able to give several incidents.) "It took devotion and faith, didn't it? And Moses was able to take that mass of people and develop them into tribes with some knowledge of God's laws so they could settle down and be God's people if they were willing to do so. Kevin, David was called in the Bible a man after God's own heart" (1 Samuel 13:14). "Do you think it was a good name for him? Did he deserve it? (Kevin should be able to give something of David's attitude toward God and of his desire to lead his people in God's way.) "Does it sometimes take courage and devotion today for grown-ups and boys and girls to lead out in God's way?" (Comments by juniors.)

"Bill, why do you think God sent Amos to Bethel? What sort of world were the king and the religious leaders building there?" (Bill should be able to point out that they were building a world far from God's ideals for people and that for a nation so to act meant it could not endure.) "Are nations today, is our nation, in danger of wrecking itself by disobeying God's laws? by paying more attention to things that are harmful than to things which are righteous?" (Let the juniors comment.)

"Sally, tell us a story of Jeremiah." (She may do so.) "Jeremiah shows us the patience as well as the courage that it takes to give God's guidance to the people. It takes a great deal of patience today, doesn't it, to tell people and tell them again and tell them over and over what God wants us to do. What would happen if people began to act as God wants them to the very first time they find out what that is?" (Let the juniors speculate a bit.)

"Charles, how was Jesus different from the messengers God had appointed before?" (The juniors should be very clear that Jesus was the Son of God and that he had come not just to tell what God wanted, but to show people what God is like and to become the Savior of the world.) "Janet, what do you like about Peter?" (Other juniors may add their ideas.)

"Ronald, what did Paul's courage do for God's work in the world?" (Ronald, and perhaps others, may be able to see that Paul's courageous work spread the gospel message far beyond the bounds it could otherwise have reached and that his letters to churches and new Christians have given us guidance for living the Christian way.) You may comment, "Some day the kingdoms of the world will become truly the kingdom of God, in which all peoples are ready and willing to act in God's ways and to make his will their will. Each of us must decide what we will do to help God's will be done in our lives."

Recreation

As prepared by the committee.

A Program for Ourselves

Different groups who have prepared various dramatizations,

pictures, and puppet shows, may give them now. Passages learned by heart, hymns learned and enjoyed may be included. You will have selected ahead of time those the juniors will like to use again.

Conducted Tour of the Exhibit

All the juniors may walk through their exhibit, while each part is commented on briefly by one pupil. Often until this moment juniors haven't got the impact of all they have done, and they enjoy this tour.

Worship Suggestions

Today's worship should be the climax of the course, whether there are guests present or not. The theme may be "Giving Praise to God." An offering may be taken for the chosen project if this has not been done. The call to worship, the hymns, scripture may be chosen from those learned. The choral reading will be an excellent thing to use. Prayers or litanies written by the juniors may be included. Be careful in choosing the hymns to have the words carry forward the thought as worship progresses. The dedication of the gifts or the offering may be a high point, as all recognize that, through the gifts they are making, it is possible for God's message to reach others as it has reached them. Gratitude for these days of study together and for the many ways in which God reveals himself and his purpose to us may be expressed. The poem, "Ships," from the pupil's book may be used with three juniors to read the verses and all reading the chorus. Later activity Sheet No. 9 may be used for pupils to draw an illustration for the poem.

Getting Ready to Take Things Home

Each junior should gather up what he is to take home, just as in the plan for when guests are present. You may have some clean-up help if you wish, or let the adult helpers take care of that.

Dismissal

You have had a wonderful time together. As you gather the juniors for a last moment together, show your delight in what they have done and in just having been together for work and play and worship during these ten sessions. Send the boys and girls off happily, with the hope that next year they can again have good times together in vacation church school.

POSSIBLE STEPS IN PLANNING

If you are having guests, your plans will have been laid before now. Your notebook will have the day scheduled. Go over the plan and be sure that all the details are taken care of so that everything will move off smoothly. Provide huge, tough, grocery bags for the juniors to take home all their souvenirs, pieces of work, donations from other juniors, and pupil's book.

If you are not having guests, your task is still to make this last session a climax, with much enjoyment and a deep sense of seeing *the whole* as well as being aware of the different parts of the study. The recall is important. You may prefer to take some time when the juniors first arrive to divide into groups and let them prepare in ten minutes something to present to the entire group when recall time comes. With younger juniors you may want to simplify the questions and statements under recall. You cannot expect quite as much from them. However, spontaneous recall is also valuable and conducted as a conversation the juniors will find satisfaction in it.

The "Program for Ourselves" will be fun, and take the place of working at the last session. It is an opportunity for the juniors to see again, hear again, take part again, in what they have specially enjoyed. The items should have been chosen as you prepared for this last day's program, and all the things necessary be ready and at hand. It should move as smoothly and promptly as a program for guests.

A guided tour of the exhibits could be another way of recall as you, or the child who is to tell about each, associates the clay tablets with Abraham's time, the time line with the whole study, the diorama's with Amos and Jeremiah, charts or posters with the men whose words are upon them. Their own commitment to try to live in God's way will be recalled with litany, use of worship books, and in other ways.

Be carefully prepared for dismantling the exhibit as each junior takes what is his to put into his bag. This may be done before worship, with worship ending the day. Or you may have worship first and then, *after* dismissal, let the juniors take their things and leave as they get ready.

APPENDIX

Registration

There are various systems of registration in use, and registration cards ask for varying items of information. But wisely managed, registration gives you information about pupils that you might otherwise not be able to get.

At the least you will need to know the name, address, telephone number, and parents' names of each junior. It is important to know his church affiliation or the fact that he is related to no church. His age and grade in school is often useful to know.

Some communities have pre-registration so that on the day you start, you can merely identify each child with the name on one of the cards, and fill in cards only for unexpected children who appear without having registered. If there has been no preregistration, one or perhaps two persons should be seated at a table with chairs ready for the juniors to occupy while the cards are being filled in. Registration is a time to get acquainted and not just an ordeal to be rushed through as fast as possible. Those who are to register pupils need to be carefully chosen for their happy disposition, carefulness, and deep interest in boys and girls.

In order to avoid waiting lines, it is wise to have activities going and to call the juniors one or two at a time from the activities, till all are registered.

As soon as each junior has registered, he may go to a second table where he may cut the edges of the "Letter to Parents" from Activity Sheet No. 1, fold it, seal it with cellophane or masking tape, and address it. It may be addressed to both parents, one parent, a grandparent, or foster parent, depending on whom he lives with. The letters should be mailed. Where there has been preregistration, the same procedure may be followed. Stamps for mailing may be supplied and put on by each child. Both recipient and juniors will pay more attention to the letter and value it more highly if it comes by mail.

If your school does not use the Activity Packet, compose a letter to parents telling about the unit of study and the planned activities. Explain how to use the pupil's book if it is to be sent home.

Name Tags

If there is a leader or any child who does not know all the rest, name tags are a *must*. One group put on just the first name or nickname and wrote it in letters an inch and a half high. The tag may be about four by eight inches and should be of tough paper (big grocery sacks are very tough) or light-weight cardboard. The juniors might like to trace the outline of large animals of Bible times, such as bear, wolf, lion, wild goat, ass, and so forth, and cut them out carefully to make the tag. Outlines of pictures of such animals should be available. (Oblong tags with crayon decorations and names written in black crayon will do.) Each junior will pin his name in place right across his chest, or across the back if learning names games are to be played.

Recreation

What would the world be like without games? They are one of the best ways of having fun together, of learning fair play and consideration for each other, of relaxing, of finding many of the values that we crave for our boys and girls.

Sometimes children have to be taught how to enjoy games fully. One vacation school group had to learn that it is fun not to cheat. Another had to learn that it is fun to take turns choosing what to play.

It is wise to have an adult referee. Disputes can often be nipped in the bud by calm suggestions. Decisions can be referred. Hot arguments about whether the ball is in or out can be eliminated. The referee may sometimes be mistaken but his word is final as every child knows.

A good game book can be found in any library.

A Quiet Competitive Game—I Went to the Zoo (for registration time):

Players choose sides and sit in two rows facing each other. Billy remarks, "I went to the zoo and I saw an eagle." Carl on the other side must match it and say, "I went to the zoo and I saw (any sort of bird)." Then Carl's side, the person sitting next to him, continues, "I went to the zoo and I saw a (naming any bird, fish, animal, insect, reptile)." Billy's next-chair neighbor must name in the same category. If any child hesitates, the referee must count up to ten, and at the count of ten that side has lost a point; the person failing merely pushes his chair back out of the line. The game goes on for points, or until most chairs have been pushed back and there are only two or three persons left. The side with most contestants remaining wins.

Time for Games

Games need not come at exactly the same time each day unless other groups use the same playground or the same equipment. For this first day, recreation may be planned by a teacher. Unless you are sure of fine weather be prepared with indoor as well as outdoor games.

After the first session a games committee may make the plans with an adult consultant. Juniors are old enough to enjoy planning a variety of recreation periods for the entire time of the vacation school. Help them think of available resources. If any one of the following is possible, plan for it at least once during the school: a swimming party; a hike; a race day (with all sorts of races from potato race to relay race); a ball game. Another thing to keep in mind is that some children need to avoid strenuous exercise in the sun and quiet games should be provided for those who prefer them.

It is well to find out what games the children themselves know and enjoy. Always stop a game before it becomes tiresome. If you stop while enjoyment is high, the juniors will want to repeat the game. Use a whistle to stop a game at the time you wish. The whistle can

121

also be used as a signal for starting races, and so on. Playtime should help the juniors learn how to co-operate not only with the plan for the day's games but with the leader, whether that is an adult or one of themselves. Sometimes such matters as honesty and fair play need to be stressed. Co-operative thinking about this may be of great value.

The Games Committee

Planning games for the second day is the immediate task, but you may have a chart ready so that games suggested can be shifted to a later day if they do not fit in for this session first planned for. Guide the juniors to think of what will give everyone fun. If everyone liked one of the games very much, it may be used again another day. Guide the committee to plan for games which alternate between strenuous and quiet. Encourage learning one new game each day. If a boy or girl is to give directions for a game, let him practice in the committee while the rest decide whether the direction is clear enough. This committee not only plans what to play, but how to manage the gametime so as to get the most from it.

Special Events

A Hike: This may be a hike to a beauty spot. It may be through a meadow, or along an irrigation ditch. It may be to someone's garden. Each hike should have a purpose. It may be to observe a natural beauty or wonder. Juniors may make mental note of such things as kinds of buildings in a town, or plants, insects, flowers, birds, rocks, or any other thing for which the region is suitable. They might even look for kinds of people, or moods of people they meet.

A Race Day: The races need to vary. They may include three-legged race; beans in a spoon race; relay races of various sorts; obstacle race; reading aloud race, timed with a stop watch; hopping race; walking a chalk line, or some other favorite race. Races should vary, too, from the strenuous to the mild.

Visitor's Day Game: A game with the juniors on one side and fathers or mothers on the other side is always popular. If the situation is such that parents cannot be there, older brothers or sisters, or the teacher group, or another section of the vacation church school may be invited to play baseball, volley ball, or even basket ball, if there is an outdoor court or a gymnasium. It will have to be a short game to fit your available time.

A Party: Giving a party for one of the younger groups is an interesting recreation possibility. Simple refreshments may be planned. Ice cream on a stick, a small cone, a couple of cookies, lemonade or some other cool drink may be provided. Choose games and features suitable for the age-group that is invited. For instance, while they may scorn "Farmer-in-the-Dell," as too babyish, they will play it gladly with little children to give them a good time. In this instance they will need to plan a number of small circles so that all the children may have a chance to be chosen. The juniors, if chosen, will need to remember to choose the small ones, not each other as the game goes on. Such a party is excellent training in thoughtfulness. It might include a tour of exhibits or a puppet show for the visitors.

A Short Dip: Sometimes a trip to a "swimming hole," or pool can be arranged. This takes careful planning, written permission from parents, the presence of someone who has had life-guard training, and full co-operation of the boys and girls. It may be a special event, after vacation school hours, but definitely a part of the program. Under any circumstance get parental permission for the trip. One school where the children did not have swimming suits, provided for boys and girls to swim in different places and all wore old clothes. On a very hot day a wading pool may be a very good bit of recreation, with the games committee inventing games that can be played in such surroundings.

A Visit to a Museum: For some groups this is a possibility. For others a visit to a church with lovely window or with a quiet sanctuary may combine recreation time with worship in that spot. It is partly a matter of timing. To pile into cars and drive to the church and back in a caravan might take up all the game time, yet be just as relaxing as playing ordinary games that day. Such a trip should, however, have the full support of the group before it is undertaken.

Worshiping Together

Informal worship can occur at any time during the teaching of a unit. Teachers should be ready with song, poem, or scripture verse to express worshipful thoughts or moods. More formal times of worship can be planned by teachers and juniors daily or for special occasions.

The setting for a worship service is important. The space should be clean, tidy, and so far as possible, made beautiful. One beautifully arranged vase of flowers is better than a dozen jammed-together bottles of carelessly chosen blooms. Even in daylight candles are lovely. A hanging behind the table on which the Bible rests centers attention and helps keep the mind away from outside sights and sounds. Quiet music is helpful. Chairs or seating arrangements should be as comfortable as possible and each junior should have space between himself and those on either side. Juniors leading in worship should have practiced so that they can speak, lead, or pray with confidence. It is better to have a few minutes for worship preparation than to interrupt worship to encourage singing, or try over again.

Suggestions are given under each session for possible development of the worship service. But it should grow out of the thoughts and feelings of the group and be the climax for the day's experiences. The adult in charge will need to be ready to change plans even at the last minute if other materials will serve the purpose better, and bring a richer feeling of closeness to God.

Juniors need to help with worship. Members of a committee can be responsible with guidance for the place of worship and its physical appointments. They can practice responses and scripture passages so as to be able to lead the group clearly and strongly. They can be ready to sing out heartily and with meaning. They should help make some choices, such as which of two hymns will mean most in a given part of the service, or whether to ask the group to learn a certain song or to memorize certain Bible passages. They may help guide others in working out a litany. They may write a prayer. Work on a worship committee is one way of training juniors to enter into worship more fully. The committee should change every three days or so.

Activity Sheet No. 6, if you have it, gives one opening arrangement of Bible verses which might be used the first few days. The juniors may want to work other verses into similar arrangements, or into something quite different. A prayer is given on one sheet. But very soon the juniors should compose a different prayer reflecting their own feelings. Hymns are suggested. There may be other well-known hymns with the same ideas that can be substituted. Or the pupils may want to take a simple tune and work out a hymn of their own. A junior group can make up a litany. Directions for doing so are given on page 128.

One possible service for the first day is given. From then on use the materials suggested to build your own form for times of worship.

Following the quiet music, which is often the music of the first hymn to be sung, you may begin worship in one of several ways.

A hymn of praise: In this hymn everyone gives praise to God, or calls on the world and people everywhere to give praise to him. Some suitable hymns of praise are:

"When Morning Gilds the Skies"

"With Happy Voices Ringing"

"Holy, Holy, Holy, Lord God Almighty"

"Come, Thou Almighty King"

"For the Beauty of the Earth"

"All People That on Earth Do Dwell"

"Maker of the Planets"

"O Worship the King"

"The God of Abraham Praise"

"Joyful, Joyful, We Adore Thee"

A Call to Worship: Often worship begins with the leader using words of the Bible or a hymn to say, "Come now, let us worship God together." Here are some Bible verses that are suitable to use as calls to worship. When a call to worship is used it may be followed by a hymn of praise either sung or said together.

Psalm 100:4-5

Psalm 100:1-2 (this, of course, must be followed by singing)

Psalm 98:4 (and this one, too)

Exodus 15:2 (a prayer could follow this)

Psalm 105:3*b*-4

Psalm 105:1-2

Psalm 95:6-7 (this must be followed by a prayer)

A Scripture Statement: Sometimes the leader does not call the rest to worship, but quotes some lovely passage of God's Word. Here are some verses which can be used in this way to begin worship:

Psalm 104:24 (this may be followed by singing "All Creatures of Our God and King")

Isaiah 55:6-7 (to be followed by a prayer)

Psalm 119:12-14

Psalm 95:3-5

A Responsive Statement: In your worship book that you may be making is one responsive statement. Here is another that could be used to open worship.

Leader: Bless the LORD, O my soul;

All: and all that is within me, bless his holy name!

124

Leader: Bless the LORD, O my
soul,

All: *and forget not all his
benefits,*

Leader: Who redeems your life
from the Pit,

All: *who crowns you with
steadfast love and
mercy,*

Leader: Bless the LORD, all his
works,

All: *in all places of his
dominion.*

*Bless the LORD, O my
soul.*

Psalm 103:1-2, 4, 22.

For Continuing Worship

You have planned for your worship program: a call to worship,
followed by a hymn or prayer; or
a hymn of praise; or a scripture
statement followed by a hymn or
prayer; or a responsive statement
followed by a hymn of praise or a
prayer.

The leader is now ready to make
a short statement which may lead
to a hymn if one has not yet been
sung, or it may lead directly to a
story or talk which will likely be
given by an adult. What is said in
this short statement gets your group
ready for the hymn or story or talk.
Study the leader's statement in the
possible worship service given in
Session 1 to see how it introduces
the hymn. Plan a similar short
statement in other services.

A story or talk may follow.
Sometimes several juniors may give
very short statements on some subject that will be helpful for everyone to think about. Here are some
subjects for short talks:

Ways of Worshiping God: By
reverent silence; by joyful singing;
by attentive listening; by thinking
about God's will; by reading from
God's Word; by speaking to him
in prayer. Six juniors could give
two or three sentences each on one
of these thoughts.

How God's Wisdom Is Shown:
By his plan for the world; by his
plan for summer and winter, seed-
time and harvest; by his plan for
families; by his giving us the
church to help us; by what we find
in the Bible. Five juniors would be
needed for this.

The Beauties of God's World:
Mountains; seas and rivers; trees,
flowers; rocks and minerals;
animals; happy children. Such subjects can be divided many ways. A
junior might say, "There are many
beautiful animals in God's world.
I saw some golden kittens playing
with each other. It was the prettiest
sight I ever saw." Another might
speak about waves on a beach or
moonlight on a lake or a waterfall.
Just one thing should be mentioned
by each junior. In such a plan all
the juniors could take part after
three or four who have prepared to
do so have set the pattern and got
things started. A junior not on the
committee might be asked to contribute when the leader said, "Do
any of the rest of you want to speak
about beauties of God's world?"

Many other subjects for short
talks by juniors will appear as your
study goes along. Watch for suggestions.

Following the story or talks or
statements, a hymn that gives everyone a chance to declare his desire
to do God's will is usually helpful.
Here are some hymns that are suitable:

"Savior, in the Words I Say"

"I Would Be True"

"Dare to Be Brave"

"The Word of God Shall Be My
Guide"

"O Master Workman of the Race"

"Father, Lead Me Day by Day"

"O Master of the Loving Heart"

"I Want to Be a Christian"

"We Plough the Fields and Scatter"

"Joy to the World"

Of course you need to choose the one that will help the boys and girls respond to the thoughts which have just been given them. Sometimes the leader needs to say a word or two between the thoughts and the singing of the hymn.

Will you take an offering? Then you need to plan for that. Here is a simple way to do it.

Call to offering: 1 Chronicles 16:29.

Music during offering: the tune of the offering hymn.

Offering hymn: "We Give Thee but Thine Own."

Of course you can substitute other things, and you may want to have a prayer of dedication instead of the offering hymn of dedication. Plan any dedication of gifts carefully.

You will find some helps and some suggestions in the study as you go along. It would be very useful for you to keep your own worship booklets with additional pages. List all the hymns, scripture passages, prayers, and ways of doing things, that you think will be helpful.

Projects for Giving

Most vacation church schools like to have a special giving project for the boys and girls. Often this is an interdenominational effort, or is something to which all denominations contribute.

There are two which can be directly related to the sending of the Bible and the Bible message to others.

1. Sending an offering to the John Milton Society.

This may be used toward getting a Bible in Braille for some blind child, or for purchasing a recording. It will not be possible to ask for a report on exactly where the money is used. But the John Milton Society,[1] will send free literature to give the juniors an idea of how their money will be spent if they send an offering.

2. Sending an offering to The American Bible Society, 430 Park Avenue, New York 22, N. Y. This gift would be used to send the scriptures, or portions of scriptures to people all over the world, and to translate into other languages the message of God to his people. Materials to help the boys and girls know what the Bible Society does will be sent on request. Order well in advance of your need.

Sending an offering to Church World Service, 475 Riverside Drive, New York 27, N. Y. This gift will be used for the relief of people all over the world—in areas of famine, war, earthquake, flood, hurricane, dire poverty and distress and to refugees. Send for information early.

4. One dollar or more will send copies of *Bible Stories and Pictures for Children Everywhere* to children around the world. For information write to World Council of Christian Education, 475 Riverside Drive, New York City 27, N. Y.

Here's How to Do It

Learning How to Handle Puppets

Boys and girls are fascinated by puppets. It is not necessary that

[1]160 Fifth Avenue, New York 10, N. Y.

they make their own, although you may want to have them do so. If you have puppets left over from previous projects or can borrow them from older boys and girls who have made them on some other occasion, or if one of your helpers is interested in preparing them ahead of time, you can use these creatively right from the beginning without taking time to make them.

Suppose the children as they come on the first day find a table with puppets on it. Someone is there to help them learn to work the puppets. They find out how to stand behind a screen or to sit on a stool below table level and to make the puppet wave its arms, walk, bow, and lie down. They find out what fun it is to make the puppets "talk" to each other.

Therefore, if you can have puppets for this first day, let the boys and girls handle them, experiment with them, and perhaps work at costuming them in costumes of Bible times.

One helper should be at the puppet center and be able to give guidance if the boys and girls need it.

Making Puppets

Perhaps you prefer to have the children make their own puppets. Activity Sheet No. 4 has clear directions for making hand puppets. Each child can follow the directions on his own sheet. *Here's How and When*[2] gives directions for making other kinds of puppets. Almost any public school teacher knows how to make puppets and one can likely be enlisted to guide such an activity. Basic Bible costumes may be

[2]See Books for Teachers, page 13.

planned, but specific characters not developed until the juniors decide on their first play.

Learning a New Song

If possible, have the tune played repeatedly as background music at various times. On the opening day it may be played, for instance, as the children register, while they are browsing around and as they work. Intersperse the music of the new song with that of other songs, familiar or to be learned later. A tune can become completely familiar to the boys and girls in this way before you begin to work with them on it.

Introduce the words with whatever you feel will interest children most. Never ask, "Would you like to learn a new song?" The negative that comes from some children as a routine response discourages the rest. "Would you like to learn . . . first, or . . . first?" gives a choice without getting a negative. Or you may simply announce, "One thing we enjoy each year is to learn new songs. This morning we are going to begin work on . . . "

An easy way to learn is to let the children read the words in unison, first stanza only. Then listen to the music, trying to fit the words to it in their minds. Then all say the words in time to the music. Then sing it. Note any phrases where the children fail to get the tune right. Go over those sections of the tune till the notes are correct. Then sing the verse.

You will find it is learned. You may follow the same procedure with succeeding verses.

Practice the hymn each day, starting with the second and then the third verse, so as to emphasize these in their turn.

Writing a Litany

A litany is a form of prayer in which the leader mentions the things for which the group wishes to pray and then the group responds with a phrase addressed to God.

Here is an example:

For all the beauty of the world, (said by the leader)

We thank thee, O God (said by the group)

For blue skies, for drifting clouds, for the sun, the stars and the moonlight,

We thank thee, O God.

The response must be suitable for the leader's words. Turn what is written above round about and it will read: We thank Thee, O God *for* (all the different things mentioned). Here are some other forms of words that can be turned around to make them into litanies. Use only one form in one litany:

We praise Thee, O God,

For all thy goodness to us.

(The leader will use as many phrases as you want to plan for. All will begin with *for* and be suitable as praise to God.)

We ask thy forgiveness, *because*

In any place where we may be, *help* us to know Thou art near, O God.

When we do not know what to do, *guide* us to know Thy way.